THE FOOD AND COOKING OF
VENICE
AND THE NORTH-EAST OF ITALY

THE FOOD AND COOKING OF
VENICE
AND THE NORTH-EAST OF ITALY

65 CLASSIC DISHES FROM VENETO, TRENTINO-ALTO ADIGE AND FRIULI-VENEZIA GIULIA

VALENTINA HARRIS

PHOTOGRAPHY BY MARTIN BRIGDALE

This edition is published by Aquamarine,
an imprint of Anness Publishing Ltd,
Hermes House, 88–89 Blackfriars Road,
London SE1 8HA
tel. 020 7401 2077; fax 020 7633 9499

www.aquamarinebooks.com
www.annesspublishing.com

If you like the images in this book and would like to
investigate using them for publishing, promotions
or advertising, please visit our website
www.practicalpictures.com for more information.

UK distributor: Book Trade Services; tel. 0116
2759086; fax 0116 2759090;
uksales@booktradeservices.com;
exportsales@booktradeservices.com

Australian agent/distributor: Pan Macmillan Australia;
tel. 1300 135 113; fax 1300 135 103;
customer.service@macmillan.com.au

New Zealand agent/distributor: David Bateman Ltd;
tel. (09) 415 7664; fax (09) 415 8892

Publisher: Joanna Lorenz
Project Editor: Kate Eddison
Copy Editors: Catherine Best and Jan Cutler
Designer: Simon Daley
Photographer: Martin Brigdale
Food Stylist: Valentina Harris
Prop Stylist: Helen Trent
Illustrator: David Cook
Indexer: Diana LeCore
Proofreading Manager: Lindsay Zamponi
Production Controller: Pirong Wang

ETHICAL TRADING POLICY
At Anness Publishing we believe that business
should be conducted in an ethical and ecologically
sustainable way, with respect for the environment
and a proper regard to the replacement of the
natural resources we employ.

As a publisher, we use a lot of wood pulp to
make high-quality paper for printing, and that wood
commonly comes from spruce trees. We are
therefore currently growing more than 750,000 trees
in three Scottish forest plantations: Berrymoss
(130 hectares/320 acres), West Touxhill (125 hectares/
305 acres) and Deveron Forest (75 hectares/
185 acres). The forests we manage contain more
than 3.5 times the number of trees employed each
year in making paper for the books we manufacture.

Because of this ongoing ecological investment
programme, you, as our customer, can have the
pleasure and reassurance of knowing that a tree is
being cultivated on your behalf to naturally replace
the materials used to make the book you are holding.

Our forestry programme is run in accordance
with the UK Woodland Assurance Scheme (UKWAS)
and will be certified by the internationally
recognized Forest Stewardship Council (FSC). The
FSC is a non-government organization dedicated to
promoting responsible management of the world's
forests. Certification ensures forests are managed in
an environmentally sustainable and socially
responsible way. For further information about this
scheme, go to www.annesspublishing.com/trees

NOTES
Bracketed terms are intended for American readers.
For all recipes, quantities are given in both metric and
imperial measures and, where appropriate, in standard
cups and spoons. Follow one set of measures, but
not a mixture, because they are not interchangeable.
• Standard spoon and cup measures are level.
1 tsp = 5ml, 1 tbsp = 15ml, 1 cup = 250ml/8fl oz.
Australian standard tablespoons are 20ml.
Australian readers should use 3 tsp in place of
1 tbsp for measuring small quantities.
• American pints are 16fl oz/2 cups. American
readers should use 20fl oz/2.5 cups in place of
1 pint when measuring liquids.
• Electric oven temperatures in this book are for
conventional ovens. When using a fan oven, the
temperature will probably need to be reduced by
about 10–20°C/20–40°F. Since ovens vary, you
should check with your manufacturer's instruction
book for guidance.
• The nutritional analysis given for each recipe is
calculated per portion (i.e. serving or item), unless
otherwise stated. If the recipe gives a range, such
as Serves 4–6, then the nutritional analysis will be
for the smaller portion size, i.e. 6 servings.
• Measurements for sodium do not include salt added
to taste.
• Medium (US large) eggs are used unless
otherwise stated.
Front cover shows Giant Beetroot and Mascarpone
Ravioli – for recipe, see page 40.

PUBLISHER'S NOTE
Although the advice and information in this book
are believed to be accurate and true at the time of
going to press, neither the authors nor the
publisher can accept any legal responsibility or
liability for any errors or omissions that may have
been made nor for any inaccuracies nor for any
loss, harm or injury that comes about from following
instructions or advice in this book.

CONTENTS

A MOUNTAINOUS REGION

The far north-eastern corner of Italy is known as Italia Nord-Orientale, a sub-region made up of Veneto, Friuli-Venezia Giulia and Trentino-Alto Adige, and is quite distinct from the rest of Italy. For the most part, locals speak their own languages, using Italian only with Italians from more southerly regions. In agriculture, cuisine and climate they are closer to Austria, Germany and Slovenia than to southern Italy, with an impressive landscape of Alpine peaks and stunning lakes.

A COOLER CLIMATE

The soaring mountain peaks that dominate most of north-eastern Italy mean cool summer temperatures and bitterly cold, often snowy winters. Only in the flat plains of the southern Veneto and along the Adriatic coast does the summer temperature and humidity rise. During the winter the cold air flows down the slopes of the Alps, the Dolomites and the Apennines and the mist rises up from the waterways of the plains. There is heavy snowfall both in the high mountains and on the lower hills, the air is often damp, the sun is rarely seen, and temperatures can barely rise above freezing for weeks on end.

This climatic pattern means that the crops grown here are very different from those usually associated with Italian food. This is not the area for tomatoes, peppers, aubergines, melons, peaches and many of the other soft fruits and delicate vegetables one associates with an Italian market. Here sturdy crops, such as cabbage, turnips, potatoes, rice, beans and maize, reign supreme, and form the basis of the local cuisine.

TOURISM AND AGRICULTURE IN THE VENETO

From the grandeur of Venice to the impressive mountains of the Dolomites, there are many sights to explore and the Veneto welcomes over 60 million tourists every year. The region is bound to the west by beautiful Lake Garda and to the north by the spectacular Dolomites. To the south-east, the region peters out in low-lying plains, river deltas and lagoons, which fringe the warm waters of the Adriatic.

The rich soil and damp climate are ideal for food production. Fields of maize and vegetables abound, as well as pasture for cattle, orchards and vineyards that grow the grapes for the delightful Prosecco wine. On the flat plains the weather can be humid in summer and cold in winter, with damp, foggy days that have become associated with the famous canals of Venice.

MOUNTAINS AND PLAINS IN FRIULI-VENEZIA GIULIA

To the far north-east of the country, the region of Friuli-Venezia Giulia borders the Veneto, Slovenia and Austria. The regional capital is Trieste, which lies in the far southern corner of the region on the

BELOW *Italia Nord-Orientale is a largely mountainous region, with flatter plains towards the Adriatic coast.*

BELOW RIGHT *Veneto, Trentino-Alto Adige and Friuli-Venezia Giulia compose the far north-eastern corner of Italy.*

Adriatic coast. Behind the Gulf of Trieste, erosion of the rocky mountains by wind and rain has created fascinating gorges, caves and underground rivers.

In northern Friuli-Venezia Giulia, the mountains rise towards the higher Alps, with precipitous passes leading into Austria and Slovenia. These high passes formed a major trading route from northern Europe to the Adriatic for hundreds of years. The region's economy is largely based on agriculture in the lower plains, with the main crops being maize, sugar beet, wheat and soy beans, as well as grapes for some wonderful, world-renowned wines. There are also many medium- and small-sized industries, making chemicals, textiles, paper and furniture.

REMOTE TRENTINO-ALTO ADIGE

This is a mountainous region, rich in rivers, streams and lakes, and divided neatly in two by the valley of the River Adige. To the west lie the remote glaciers of the Adamello-Presanella-Care Alto and Brenta mountain ranges. To the east the ranges of Lagorai, Latemar, the Dolomites of Fassa and the Pale di San Martino rise majestically. The biggest lake is the famous Lake Garda, and there are 297 lakes in Trentino. Most of them are hidden high in the mountains at over 1,500m/5,000ft above sea level.

Extensive dark coniferous forests cover the slopes of the mountains, and three natural parks help to preserve the typical animals and vegetation of the Alpine environment, including the now rare wild bear. The pleasantly warm and green valleys nestling between the mountain peaks are ideal for growing orchard fruit and grapes for some world-class wines, such as a splendid Cabernet Sauvignon. The main industry here is tourism, with excellent winter ski resorts transforming themselves into centres for hiking in the beautiful countryside in the summer.

ABOVE LEFT *The beautiful Lake Garda is a world-famous tourist destination.*

ABOVE *Farmhouses nestle in the vineyards of the Veneto, where grapes are grown to make the delectable Prosecco wine.*

BELOW *Horses roam on a plateau in the province of Bolzano, overlooked by the beautiful Italian Dolomites.*

THE BORA

The strong wind known as the Bora blows in violent gusts along the coastal areas of Friuli-Venezia Giulia, especially in the province of Trieste. Buildings in several towns and villages in these parts have stones permanently placed on their roofs to prevent their roof tiles from being blown off. Chains and ropes are stretched along the sidewalks in downtown Trieste to help pedestrians to walk safely when the wind tries to lift them off their feet.

A GLORIOUS HISTORY

The north-east of Italy contains many of the country's most precious treasures. It is a sumptuous area full of world-renowned natural beauty and man-made wonders, from the soaring peaks of the Dolomites and the lush flatlands of the southern Veneto to historic Verona and majestic Venice, the ultimate city of canals, gondolas and romance. Austrian-style buildings dot the mountainous northern landscape, contrasting with the more typical Roman ruins, which remind us of the centuries-long tug of war over control of these rich regions.

AN ANCIENT CULTURE

North-eastern Italy, from the Adriatic Sea to the eastern Alps, is situated in a strategic position at the main crossroads between the Mediterranean and northern Europe. It is known to have been inhabited before the first Bronze Age people settled there around 2000 BC. Later, the peaceful Veneto people began to cultivate the land. They lived beside the rivers in wooden dwellings similar to the present-day casoni of the Veneto lagoon, and were dedicated to farming, fishing, bronze-work and the breeding of horses.

THE ROMAN EMPIRE

Once Roman influence spread to north-eastern Italy, there followed a prosperous period of about 300 years that favoured the arts and architecture, peaceful agriculture and trade. Unfortunately, after the fall of the Roman Empire in AD 476, the region was invaded and plundered by barbarian hordes. The populations of the destroyed cities took refuge in the coastal lagoons and established new towns such as Venice, Chioggia, Caorle and Grado.

THE RISE OF VENICE

Venice began its historical adventure on the seas, regularly having to defend itself against attacks from Franks, Slavs, Hungarians and Normans. Trade flourished between Constantinople (now Istanbul), Egypt, the Holy Land and northern Europe and ensured the city's prestige and riches. From 1500 to 1800, Venice was at the height of grandeur, though it was often attacked by other European states, jealous of its power and prosperity. Furthermore, there was an ongoing war against the Turks of the Ottoman Empire, with whom the Venetians fought and traded at the same time.

The arts enjoyed a Golden Age during these years, and painting, architecture, literature and music all thrived. However, the city was in an inexorable and slow decline, which was largely concealed until the arrival of Napoleon, who brutally put an end to the Venetian Republic, plundering it, then handing it over to Austria. For approximately 60 years the Veneto remained under Austrian rule, but not without some epic battles, during which the Venetians fought valiantly to defend their beautiful city.

RIGHT *Wooden casoni perch on the edge of the Venetian lagoon; a reminder of the traditional wooden dwellings used by early fishing communities.*

DECLINE AND REVIVAL

After 1866 the Veneto region became part of the Kingdom of Italy, but an economic crisis, followed by two World Wars, caused a serious depression in this mainly agricultural region. This was also the cause of the large-scale emigration, when so many Venetian people sought a better life in Argentina, Brazil, the United States, northern Europe, Canada, Australia and other countries of the world, where their hard-working ethic always stood them in good stead.

It was only in the 1960s that the Veneto really started to come alive again. Thanks to new commercial opportunities and the industriousness of its people, mainly in the sectors of machinery, wood, furniture, footwear, clothing, agriculture and wines, the Veneto has returned to being a commercially successful bridge between the Mediterranean and the rest of Europe.

VENICE'S NEIGHBOURING REGIONS

The adjoining region to the east, Friuli-Venezia Giulia, suffered most during the centuries of Venetian domination. The dangers of living in the Friulian plain, with great barbarian invasions passing through after the collapse of the Roman Empire, drove many people to seek shelter on the islands in the lagoons or in fortified hilltop villages, causing a general depopulation of the more fertile parts of the region and consequent impoverishment. For centuries, warring armies marched across the countryside and breeding animals were used to feed the soldiers. Venetian boat-builders also chopped down most of the trees that covered the Friulian plain to make bigger, better ships. Even after World War II, the region was unstable: much of the area was claimed by what was then Yugoslavia, and Friuli-Venezia Giulia was not incorporated as part of Italy until

1963. Many of its towns still bear the signs of both Austrian and Slovenian influence in lifestyle, language, folklore and cuisine.

To the north of Venice and the Veneto, Trentino-Alto Adige was more influenced by Austria and the Habsburg Empire, just on the other side of the mountains. This whole area has been conquered and re-conquered so many times that it feels as though it is part of both Italy and Austria at the same time; both languages are spoken, as well as several local dialects. Today, particularly in the northern part of the region, Alto Adige (or Südtirol), there is still an obvious northern European flavour, with street signs in German and Italian, Austrian architecture, and Austrian or German dishes on the menu in the restaurants.

ABOVE LEFT *Austrian-style architecture is visible in the mountainous areas of northern Trentino-Alto Adige, serving as a reminder of the proximity and influence of Austria.*

ABOVE *The beautiful city of Verona sits on the winding river Adige.*

BELOW *Boats line the canals of the world-famous city of Venice.*

A HEARTY CUISINE

The climate, landscape and history of the north-eastern corner of Italy have all contributed to create dishes that are very different to those of the Mediterranean south. Staples of the Italian menu, such as pasta, pizza, tomatoes and mozzarella, are very hard to find. Pasta is largely replaced by rice and polenta, and a great deal of meat is eaten, especially pork, game and poultry. The food tends to be creamy and rich, providing perfect warming sustenance for the population during the cold winters.

THE INFLUENCE OF NORTHERN EUROPE

German, Austrian, Slovenian and Hungarian influences are very evident in these regions, and ingredients such as paprika, horseradish, cumin and cinnamon are common. In the Veneto, Venice's tradition of trading with other nations around the world gives a cosmopolitan feel to the cuisine. One really notable difference between this area of Italy and regions further south is in the kind of bread baked for daily consumption. Here, bread tends to be dark and chewy, often made with rye, giving it a very Germanic flavour and texture. It looks and tastes extremely different from the famous light Italian breads, such as focaccia, or the full-flavoured crusty loaves that hail from Puglia and Tuscany.

THE RURAL FOOD OF THE VENETO

The low plains of the Po, Adige and Piave rivers supply livestock, rice for risotto and corn for polenta. Higher up, in the hills that rise towards the Alps around Lake Garda, game and wild mushrooms abound. These slopes have the perfect climate for curing prosciutto, salami and cheeses,

and growers produce some splendid wine such as Bardolino, Valpolicella, Soave and Prosecco. The two best-known dishes of the Veneto region are risi e bisi, a creamy risotto with peas, Parmesan and pancetta, and pasta e fagioli, a very thick bean, pasta and vegetable soup.

Polenta, beans and rice form the solid basis of the local diet throughout the Veneto, rather than pasta. Inland, the main protein is meat, including beef, pork and game, which is often made into goulash, following the traditions of the Austro-Hungarian Empire. In the inland valleys, some of Italy's finest sharp cheeses are produced, such as Asiago and the lesser-known Monte Veronese.

Fish is also popular inland, far away from the coast, where there are traditional dishes using freshwater fish such as trout and eel, and also baccalà (salted white fish that lasts for many months). Perhaps the most famous sweet cake of the Veneto region is the tall, star-shaped pandoro, which comes from the city of Verona, and makes a light alternative to the richer panettone from Lombardia.

BELOW *The marshy flatlands of the Po Delta are an excellent place to catch eels, as well as being an area of outstanding natural beauty.*

BELOW RIGHT *Grapes for some of Italy's finest wines are grown in north-eastern Italy.*

The traditional simple country cuisine of the Veneto is a far cry from the rich and varied dishes found in Venice, which has for centuries been able to use ingredients shipped here from many far-flung corners of the world. Trade with the Arabs led to the introduction of rice, which rapidly became a dominant element in the regional diet in the form of creamy risotto. Venetian traders also brought baccalà and stockfish from the chilly north to add to the vast range of food available in this cosmopolitan city.

Fresh produce from the sea The region's proximity to the Adriatic means that fresh fish and shellfish are an important part of the Veneto diet, and all the treasures of the sea are available, from crabs such as moleche and spider crab to sardines and squid. The Venetian speciality, sarde in saor, is a sweet-and-sour dish of cooked, lightly pickled sardines. Another favourite is risotto al nero, a dramatic dish of black squid and soft risotto rice. Eels are extremely popular and abundant in the marshy areas of the Po Delta.

Local specialities Treviso is reputedly the place where the famous Italian dessert called tiramisù was first invented, but the town and province are also very well known for the prized radicchio Trevisano. This variety of red-leaved chicory has long, elegant leaves, and is used in many dishes, both sweet and savoury, even to flavour grappa. The region has been producing this much sought-after vegetable for over a thousand years. Asparagus is also popular in its short season, particularly the white asparagus of Bassano in the Veneto.

FRIULI-VENEZIA GIULIA: GERMANIC FOOD
With Slovenia on its eastern border and Austria to the north, it is not at all surprising to see the influences of these countries in Friuli-Venezia Giulia. As a direct result of its long connection with the Austro-Hungarian Empire, the cuisine focuses on sauerkraut, potatoes, turnips, and savoury and sweet strudels, with an intriguing local boiled variation called strucolo. Friuli-Venezia Giulia boasts many other sweet cakes and desserts, including

ABOVE *White asparagus, a delicacy of Bassano, is displayed at markets throughout the Veneto.*

LEFT *Fresh fish and shellfish are sold each morning at the famous Rialto fish market in Venice.*

ABOVE LEFT *Alpine cows graze on the rugged mountain landscape of north-eastern Italy.*

ABOVE RIGHT *Polenta is traditionally cooked over an open fire in Trentino-Alto Adige.*

gubana, a spicy sweet bread with grappa. Spices such as paprika, poppy seeds, cinnamon, cumin and horseradish are used daily, and rice or polenta feature on the menu instead of pasta. The local speciality, frico, is seasoned, salty cheese, cut into pieces and fried in butter. This is sometimes served with polenta, but can also be eaten on its own.

Friuli-Venezia Giulia is well known for its barley fields, and the locals are fond of using this grain to make orzotto, which is similar to risotto. The chilly winter weather means that warming soups such as la jota are especially welcome, based on beans, greens and pork ribs, with some tasty pork fat. Another significant characteristic of the region is that tomatoes are rarely used, which radically changes the colour, texture and taste of the local food compared to that found in southern Italy.

Well-flavoured meat dishes The custom of lightly smoking cold cuts of meat, especially prosciutto, is common here but not in other parts of Italy.

SPECIALITIES FROM TRIESTE

Cooking in Trieste reflects the Venetian style, combined with strong Austrian and Slavic influences. The main specialities are the local brodetto, a fish soup, and mesta, a kind of polenta cooked in water and milk, also eaten with fish. Trieste has a tradition of delightful literary cafés; the last of these to survive is the famous San Marco café in Via Battisti.

There is an abundance of strong-flavoured wild game in the inland areas and some very good beef from the cattle raised on the plains bordering the Adriatic. Many delicious local sausages are made, as well as excellent cured ham from San Daniele, in the province of Udine, which rivals the best Parma ham in flavour and quality. Another favourite is the rich and tasty smoked ham called speck that is made both here and in neighbouring Trentino-Alto Adige.

Flowery white wines Friuli-Venezia Giulia produces some of the best Italian white wines, many of which are wonderfully light and refreshing, and are made with Germanic grape varieties such as Riesling and Müller-Thurgau. One unusual speciality is Picolit, an extraordinary sweet wine developed in the 1700s as a substitute for the sought-after Hungarian wine, Tokay, which was prevented by war from reaching Europe's courts.

TRENTINO-ALTO ADIGE: WARMING FOOD
The landlocked region of Trentino-Alto Adige includes the lofty Dolomite Mountains in the north and east, and pleasantly undulating hills awash with vineyards and orchards in the south. Freshwater fish, pork, game, dairy produce, vegetables and fruit are basic elements of the simple local cuisine. Germanic and Hungarian influences are evident in the tasty dumplings, thick soups flavoured with caraway seeds, smoked ham, light pastry strudels of various kinds and the liberal use of sauerkraut. German-type sausages are very

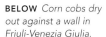
the burning wood adds a slightly smoky taste to the polenta bubbling in the pot. Basic polenta can take on another flavour altogether with the addition of some dark Saracen corn, and becomes polenta nera, black polenta.

Delicious dumplings Large dumplings called canederli are made out of stale bread, eggs, flour and milk, with the addition of chopped bacon, salami, liver and cabbage or spinach. These dumplings are simply boiled in a clear broth or water. A sweet version is made with the same basic bread and egg mixture, but with a prune in the centre, and the whole thing is dipped in breadcrumbs. Other dumpling-type dishes include small gnocchi flavoured with spinach, known as spinatspätzle, which are often served as an accompaniment to goulash.

Sweet treats Cakes and pastries play an important role in this cold climate. Favourites include strudel, which are often filled with apples and spiced with cinnamon, or zelten, which are similar pastries filled with walnuts and dried fruits. The wild berries that grow in the woods and meadows of the region are often used in the local desserts, as well as being turned into delicious liqueurs.

WILD PRODUCE FROM THE HILLS

The lively street market in Trento spills over with wonderful local produce, especially in the summer and autumn. Many of the 250 varieties of wild mushrooms found in the mountains and hills can be bought here in season. So important is the local passion for mushrooms that some policemen are trained to identify the different varieties, allowing uncertain foragers to get their precious findings checked by an expert.

popular, especially when served with beer and sauerkraut, or sweet fruity chutney. Big, hearty soups are made with barley and speck, and there is a tasty local version of a Swiss rösti, a crisp pancake of grated potatoes and chopped bacon. The emphasis of the cuisine is always on hearty, strong-tasting food made to sustain the population through the cold weather.

Polenta – the staple food The most fundamental element of the cuisine of Trentino is polenta, which consists of ground maize meal, boiled in salted water and stirred constantly until it has thickened into a kind of porridge (oatmeal). There are many different ways to enjoy polenta: it is often served warm and soft with local cheeses melting on top, or as an accompaniment to a meal such as game stew, baccalà (salted cod) or beans. It is traditionally cooked over an open fire, so that

BELOW *Corn cobs dry out against a wall in Friuli-Venezia Giulia.*

FESTIVALS AND CELEBRATIONS

Across the north-east of Italy, a multitude of festivals take place that feature local food, wines or beers, or mark religious days in traditional fashion. These occur everywhere from small mountain villages and countryside towns to the large cities of Venice, Verona, Vicenza, Treviso and Padova. The origins of some of these traditions are buried in the distant past. The one thing that they have in common is that they all provide an opportunity to celebrate with plenty of good food and wine.

THE CARNIVAL OF VENICE

Carnival time in Venice is a world-famous annual celebration that takes place every February and is still, after more than 900 years, one of the highlights of the Venetian calendar. At this time of year, with the early spring sunlight sparkling on the water after the damp and foggy winter, revellers enjoy sweet, sustaining snacks. This is when a huge range of deep-fried pastries and desserts really come into their own. They were traditionally served as street snacks for the carnival revellers and include deep-fried squares of custard, crema fritta, and many other delicious local specialities.

The tradition of wearing masks at carnival time in the city of Venice has ancient origins and has grown in popularity. At one time, masks were worn by the inhabitants of the city for many months of the year. They were sometimes used to conceal the faces of people picking pockets, gambling or begging on street corners, as well as those intent on more innocent escapades such as creeping undetected into a lover's house. These masks are now sold in their millions as popular tourist souvenirs, and are still worn today in the narrow streets of Venice during carnival time.

VINITALY

This is the annual international wine show in Verona, which takes place in April. Here, many Italian and international exhibitors gather to promote their best production in an overview of vine-growing and winemaking traditions.

THE VOGALONGA (HISTORICAL REGATTA)

This boat race, begun in the 1970s by a group of rowing enthusiasts, takes place each May, traditionally on Ascension Day, on the canals and lagoon of Venice and is one of the most important events on the Venetian calendar. It is a fun and non-competitive event in which any type of rowing boat is welcome to participate and every entrant gets a prize.

SAN DANIELE PROSCIUTTO FESTIVAL

Each June, the town of San Daniele del Friuli in the region of Friuli-Venezia Giulia celebrates its famous prosciutto crudo. For three days, the streets are full of stalls where locals and visitors can sample the delights of the wonderful cured ham in a variety of local speciality dishes. There are a whole host of festivities, including traditional singing and dancing in the streets.

BELOW *The beautiful masks of Venice are now a world-famous symbol of the February carnival celebrations.*

BELOW RIGHT *An annual pumpkin festival takes place in Bolzano, in Trentino-Alto Adige.*

Throughout this northern region, in the best Austrian tradition, delightful Christmas markets spring up from early November, ending on Twelfth Night, 6 January. These markets sell all the local specialities, including delicious sweet pastries and cakes.

SAN VALENTINO FESTIVAL

The small village of San Valentino, near Trento, in Trentino-Alto Adige hosts a wonderful cheese-rolling contest each June to celebrate the local produce of this Alpine region. There is also a sausage-eating and beer-drinking competition, reflecting the Austrian influences of this area.

FESTA DEL REDENTORE

One of the most important summer festivals in Venice is the Festa del Redentore (Feast of the Redeemer), based on thanksgiving for the end of the bubonic plague in 1575, which killed tens of thousands of Venetian citizens. A week of celebrations leads up to the third Sunday in July, when there is a huge street party around the Franciscan church of the Redentore on the island of Giudecca, with church services, a regatta, bands, fireworks and, of course, the obligatory feasting in the streets.

RISOTTO FESTIVAL

Just south of Verona, the village of Isola della Scala hosts an unmissable festival celebrating Veronese rice from mid-September to mid-October. During the festival, a multitude of delicious rice dishes are cooked and served, and there are tours of rice fields, events for children, concerts and gastronomic competitions.

MERANO INTERNATIONAL WINE FESTIVAL

Taking place every November in the province of Bolzano, this is the second most important food and wine festival after Vinitaly. More than 400 winemakers and over 120 food producers gather together to show the very best of local produce.

FAMILY CELEBRATIONS

Although not as strictly Catholic as the south of Italy, baptisms, first communions and weddings are important celebrations for many families in the north-eastern region. Huge amounts of money are spent on lavish weddings with hundreds of guests, and the meal that is served is of the utmost importance. Each guest will receive a small gift with some sugared almonds attached, known as bomboniera.

ABOVE *An Austrian-style Christmas market takes place each year in the city of Trento, in Trentino-Alto Adige.*

LEFT *Traditional dancing takes place in San Daniele, in Friuli-Venezia Giulia, to celebrate the annual festival of the famous local ham.*

CLASSIC INGREDIENTS

The three regions of Veneto, Trentino-Alto Adige and Friuli-Venezia Giulia, tucked into the north-eastern corner of Italy, have their own micro-climate, their own crops and, consequently, their own traditional dishes. Southern Italy may boast the ideal conditions for growing olives, citrus fruits and durum wheat for pasta; but this colder northern area is the perfect place to grow root vegetables, rice, beans and maize, and to raise strong, healthy cattle for meat and dairy produce. This has led to a cuisine of hearty, wholesome dishes that warm and sustain the population during the cold Alpine winters. Influences from neighbouring European countries, such as Austria, Germany, Hungary and Slovenia, are noticeable in the ingredients and dishes.

ROOT VEGETABLES

The damp, misty weather that prevails over most of north-eastern Italy certainly does not allow for growing the sun-ripened vegetables that people usually associate with Italy, such as aubergines (eggplants), tomatoes and (bell) peppers. On the other hand, crops of more hearty, earthy ingredients, such as potatoes, turnips and cabbage, do thrive in the cool weather conditions.

Potatoes feature a great deal in the local cuisine, as a side dish, for making dumplings and gröstl (the local version of rösti), and to thicken soups and stews. Cabbage is usually used to make sauerkraut, very much a northern European delicacy, which is added to soups such as la jota and is also served as a vegetable with pork dishes and sausages. This is just about the only part of Italy

where turnips are grown and used in cooking, either as an accompanying vegetable or as an ingredient in soups and stews.

SPECIALITY VEGETABLES

As well as these sturdy root vegetables, there are some interesting crops that are not found in other areas of Italy. Pumpkins are popular all over north-eastern Italy, but especially in Veneto, where they are used to make cakes, risotto and soups among many other dishes. The most highly prized variety of pumpkin is the knobbly Barrucca pumpkin that is grown in the Chioggia area.

Different varieties of bitter, red-leaved chicory are grown in the Veneto region, such as the loose-leaved Verona and the tightly packed Chioggia variety. However, neither of these is as much in

BELOW, LEFT TO RIGHT
Beetroot, cabbage and pumpkin.

demand as the elegant, long-leaved variety, called radicchio Trevisano, which is grown in and around Treviso.

White asparagus is a delicacy often found in Germany and other northern European countries. It is grown in Bassano del Grappa, in the Veneto.

Vivid crimson beetroot (beet) is often used in the cooking of Veneto, Trentino-Alto Adige and Friuli-Venezia Giulia, as a side dish, a soup or stew ingredient, or pickled to serve alongside cured meats or cheese.

FRUIT AND NUTS

Orchard fruits and berries predominate in the cool climate of north-eastern Italy. The Val di Non, in Trentino-Alto Adige, produces most of the apple crop for the whole of Italy. Locally they are used to make the famous apfelstrudel as well as a variety of other Austrian-style cakes and pastries. Pears also feature prominently in the cuisine of this area, and in the Veneto in particular, where they are used in a variety of desserts, such as pear and amaretti tarts.

In Friuli-Venezia Giulia and Trentino-Alto Adige, woodland berries such as wild myrtleberries (whortleberries), raspberries, redcurrants, blackcurrants and other soft fruits are used in both sweet and savoury dishes. Dried fruits – raisins and sultanas (golden raisins) in particular – feature in savoury recipes, such as bean and raisin polenta,

as well as sweet dishes, such as the delicious little deep-fried Venetian fritters made of yeast dough. Of all the nuts that are grown in these regions, almonds are certainly the favourite. They crop up in a multitude of recipes, from polenta cake to the spicy sweet bread known as gubana, which is a popular recipe in Trieste.

SPICES, HERBS AND FLAVOURINGS

The influence of Venetian traders can be seen in the use of cumin, cinnamon and paprika. Cumin, with its strong aromatic flavour, is used to enhance grappa and bread, and is added to soups and stews; cinnamon is a sweeter spice, most often found in cakes or biscuits (cookies); and vivid

HORSERADISH

The hot, bitter root of horseradish is not usually associated with Italian cuisine, and is used very rarely throughout the country as a whole. Here, however, in the north-eastern corner, especially in Trentino-Alto Adige and Friuli-Venezia Giulia, it is made into a strong-tasting, spicy condiment to accompany meat dishes. The only other region where it may be used in Italian cooking is Basilicata, in the far south, where it has earned the name 'poor man's truffle'.

BELOW, LEFT TO RIGHT
Raisins, garlic and sage.

ABOVE, LEFT TO RIGHT
Asiago cheese, pancetta, scallops and yellow polenta.

orange-red paprika blends beautifully with game or other meat in a stew. These warming spices are rarely found further south in Italy.

Many garden herbs are used in daily cooking, but perhaps the most popular is flat leaf parsley, which is used as a garnish and as an integral flavouring ingredient to many dishes. Garlic, of course, is another firm favourite, as it is in the other regions of Italy.

DAIRY PRODUCE
Milk, cream and butter are used extensively in the cooking of north-eastern Italy, and give a creamy, fat-rich quality to the local cuisine. The most important cheese of the region is Asiago, a sharp cheese made in the Veneto that is usually relished on its own, although it is sometimes used for cooking. Other local cheeses are made from milk produced in the high Alpine pastures, where the air is cold and clear, and these cheeses tend to be high in fat. Cheeses from Trentino include the sweet Algunder Bauernkäse Halbfett and the more robust, sharp Algunder Butterkäse. A low-fat but very tasty local cheese does exist: it is known as Almkäse but is very rare and difficult to find outside of the region.

MEAT, POULTRY AND GAME
In these three regions, pork, beef and horsemeat are the most common meats, as well as wild game, such as venison. Pork fat is often used for cooking

instead of olive oil or butter. In Veneto people eat a lot of poultry, including duck, chicken and chicken livers, guinea fowl, turkey and goose. Poultry tends to be simply roasted, fried or grilled (broiled), or chopped and mixed into a risotto.

The most famous of the locally produced cured meats are the delicate prosciutto di San Daniele, which is cured in the province of Udine, and the smoked ham known as speck. There are plenty of different types of hearty, tasty sausage from Friuli-Venezia Giulia and Trentino-Alto Adige, as well as some varieties of salami that are traditionally made in the Veneto.

FISH AND SHELLFISH
Fish is just as much a part of the local menu in these regions as meat, poultry or game. A vast range of fish dishes are an important part of the

---

CARPACCIO

The Veneto is the region where the famous dish Carpaccio was first created. It consists of paper-thin slices of raw veal, laid flat on a plate and scattered with shavings of fresh Parmesan, then dressed with lemon juice and olive oil. The term Carpaccio has come to refer to any fruit or vegetable, not just meat, which is sliced very thinly.

local cuisine. Common ingredients include the plentiful freshwater fish from the lakes, marshes and rivers, such as trout and eel; fresh fish and shellfish from the Adriatic sea, such as herrings, sardines, squid and crab; as well as stockfish (dried cod) and baccalà (salted cod). All of these fish and shellfish are used to make fantastic soups, risottos, casseroles and stews, often served alongside polenta.

GRAINS AND BEANS

The favourite carbohydrates in these three regions are rice and polenta, and people here only rarely eat pasta. Other grains, such as rye, oats and buckwheat, are also added to bread, soups or cakes. Rice is not only the star of the dish risotto, it is also found in soup to add bulk, and can even be added to an unusual frittata with bacon and chopped vegetables.

Beans form a major part of the diet, especially the much-loved local variety, fagiolo di Lamon. Lamon beans are grown exclusively in the province of Belluno and are very precious to the cooks of this region. There are four different kinds of Lamon bean, which differ in shape and size, but which are all protected by official trade descriptions. These beans need a long, slow cooking process to make them tender, so they often appear in thick soups or casseroles, with or without the inclusion of meat.

SALSA PEVERADA

This is a Venetian sauce to serve with roast game, duck or chicken. It may seem quite peculiar to blend the flavours of this sauce with the already very intense taste of game, but it works surprisingly well. Although the sauce is created specifically for roasted game, it is also fabulous with a plain roasted chicken and wonderful with duck.

SERVES 4

3 anchovy fillets, boned and finely chopped
115g/4oz chicken livers, trimmed and finely chopped
2 rashers (strips) unsmoked lean back bacon,
   very finely chopped
grated rind of l lemon
1 garlic clove, peeled
90ml/6 tbsp olive oil
15ml/1 tbsp white wine vinegar
sea salt and ground black pepper

1 Put the anchovy fillets into a small pan and add the chicken livers, bacon, lemon rind, garlic and olive oil.

2 Cook over a low heat, stirring frequently, for about 15 minutes, or until soft and cooked through. The texture of the sauce should be as smooth as possible.

3 Remove and discard the clove of garlic. Sprinkle the sauce with the white wine vinegar, season it with salt and pepper, then stir it well. Serve the sauce hot.

ABOVE, LEFT TO RIGHT
Cinnamon and nutmeg, pine nuts, and candied fruits and walnuts.

SWEET THINGS

Many of the local cakes and pastries in Veneto, Trentino-Alto Adige and Friuli-Venezia Giulia are very similar to those found in neighbouring Slovenia and Austria. The most well-known regional delicacies include a German- or Austrian-style strudel and a sweet, fruity bread, which is known as gubana. The best place to find these delicious cakes is in Trieste in Trentino-Alto Adige, a city known for its cafés and pastry shops. Here, there are many different pastries of Austrian or Hungarian origin with names such as putizza, presnitz or rigojancsi.

In all three regions, the fiery clear alcoholic spirit, grappa, is often used in baking, both for cakes and for pastries as well as for soaking dried fruits, such as sultanas (golden raisins), before adding them to the other ingredients.

In Trentino-Alto Adige, wild berries and soft fruits are used to make delectable tarts, local apples go into Austrian-inspired apple pastries, sweet fritters called fëies da marmulada are filled with jam, and sweet dumplings, known as canederli, are stuffed with prunes or dried apricots in a typical dessert recipe of Bolzano.

In the Alpine areas, cakes and pastries are sometimes made using buckwheat or polenta flour, and this is the only region of Italy where you might occasionally find rhubarb in regional cakes and tarts.

ALCOHOLIC DRINKS

Many kinds of alcoholic drinks are made in these regions, both for local consumption and for national and international export. A glass of wine naturally goes with a good meal, but beer is gaining in popularity and is also used as an ingredient in rich, flavoursome stews.

Wine The production of wine occurs in all three of these north-eastern regions, but the best vineyards tend to be in Friuli-Venezia Giulia and the Veneto, where the flatter landscape is more suitable for growing grapes than the high hills and mountains that make up much of Trentino-Alto Adige. Trentino does, however, produce a delicious red wine called Teroldego, as well as a few interesting white wines. The most unusual wines from this region are the extremely special Moscato Rosa, or Rosenmuscateller, which is a sweet rosé wine from the Alto Adige area, and Lagrein, which comes in both a red and a very dark rosé version.

Friuli-Venezia Giulia has built an enviable reputation in Italy and abroad for white wines made by relatively small independent estates. The whites have long been dominated by Tocai Friuliano; recently the European Court ruled that Tocai must change its name so as not to be confused with the sweet dessert wine, Tokay, which comes from Hungary.

The Veneto region has emerged in recent times as Italy's largest producer of wine, making more than 300 million bottles each year. Leading the flow is Verona's trio of world-famous wines: Soave, Valpolicella and Bardolino. These are closely followed by Prosecco, the light sparkling wine from the Conegliano area, which is growing in popularity elsewhere in Italy as well as across the rest of the world.

Beer It is hardly surprising to find that beer is extremely popular in the north-eastern area of Italy, owing to its close geographical and historical links with Austria and other northern European countries. Beer is enjoyed both as a drink to accompany food and as an ingredient in a great many dishes throughout the entire area. Using beer in cooking is especially apparent in the cuisine of Friuli-Venezia Giulia. The most important brewery in the region is the world-renowned Moretti, which, to this day, still works to a traditional recipe that has changed very little since it was founded in 1859.

Grappa The strong, clear distilled spirit known as grappa is between 37.5% and 60% alcohol by volume. It is made by distilling the grape residue (mainly the skins, but also including the stems and seeds) left over from winemaking after pressing. Some grappa, known as prima uva, is made with

---

HERBAL LIQUEURS

The Val Gardena, in Trentino-Alto Adige, is renowned for being the best area in Italy for the production of herbal liqueurs. Juniper, gentian, rhubarb and wild Alpine flowers are all distilled to make a range of very special drinks to round off a meal. The grappa from this region is also highly prized and has acquired world recognition for its purity and high quality.

---

the whole grapes. The flavour of grappa, like that of wine, depends on the type and quality of the grape used as well as the fine details of the distillation process.

In Italy, grappa is primarily served as a digestivo, or after-dinner drink, where its main purpose is to aid the digestion of a heavy meal. Grappa may also be added to espresso coffee to create a caffè corretto, which translates as 'corrected coffee'. Another variation of this is ammazza caffè, literally meaning 'coffee-killer', where the espresso is drunk first, followed by a few drops of grappa served in its own glass. In the Veneto, after finishing a cup of espresso with sugar, a few drops of grappa are poured into the nearly empty cup, swirled, and drunk down in one mouthful. This is known in local dialect as resentin.

BELOW, LEFT TO RIGHT
Chocolate, pears and red wine.

SOUPS AND ANTIPASTI
ZUPPE, MINESTRE E ANTIPASTI

In this north-eastern corner of Italy, where the winters are cold, it is no wonder a lot of nourishing soups pepper the local menus. Hearty ingredients and flavoursome stocks create warming, nutritious broths. Antipasti are practically synonymous with Venice and the surrounding regions. Venetians have a habit of snacking on the go, usually with a glass of Prosecco, which dates back many centuries. These little snacks are called cichetti, and they are eaten before lunch or before dinner – in Venice this is a way of life. It is an extension of the concept of antipasti, a social activity where the day's events are discussed as the wine is sipped and the food consumed.

RIB-STICKING SOUPS AND WHIPPED SALT COD

Little nibbles are a wonderful way to begin any meal and are also perfect finger food to serve at the many parties that Venetians love to throw. They can be a golden pile of crispy fried sardines, served hot, with just a squeeze of lemon. Or a piece of toasted bread, spread with a dollop of baccalà mantecato, softened salt cod whipped into a creamy mousse-like texture with olive oil and often flavoured with herbs and garlic. The incredibly sweet and delicate Prosciutto di San Daniele is wonderful just served simply on its own as an appetizer. This ham, when whole, is easy to distinguish from Parma ham or any other kind of cured ham because it is sold with the trotter still attached to the end of the haunch. In Friuli, a popular antipasto is Frico, a lacy galette of fried local cheese, crisp and pale, and utterly moreish.

While antipasti may be fine fare for the hot summer days, once autumn has ushered in the cool weather it is robust and substantial soups that take pride of place in the homes of these regions. It is hard to really believe how cold it can get in this north-eastern corner of Italy unless you have experienced it for yourself. The biting wind that sweeps down from the mountains towards the coast makes Venice an extremely chilly destination for even the hardiest of tourists in the depths of winter. Up in the mountains, it couldn't feel any further away from the sun-scorched southern regions of Italy. The locals prepare for the harsh winter by stockpiling their woodsheds during the summer months. The regional soups are prepared using a wide variety of ingredients that are guaranteed to help keep out the chill, including plenty of beans, potatoes, rice and pork.

DOGE'S SOUP
ZUPPA DEI DOGI

This dish is based on a very old recipe from the kitchens of the Doge's Palace in Venice. It is supposed to represent all the beauty and riches of Venice with the intense colours of precious stones reflected in the beetroot, carrot and courgette. The little golden rice balls represent Venice's great wealth, and especially that of the Doge's Palace, and are intended as a reminder of Venice in all her glory, with sunlight glinting off the water and the golden orbs of the churches.

1 Cook the rice in boiling water to cover for 10 minutes, or until still quite firm. Drain the rice and transfer to a bowl.

2 Add the Fontina cheese to the rice and mix until well blended. Add the egg, Parmesan and olive oil. Mix thoroughly and shape into walnut-sized balls. Chill until required.

3 Bring the meat stock to the boil in a pan and add the beetroot, carrot, potato and courgette matchsticks.

4 Simmer the vegetables for 5 minutes. Do not allow them to cook any longer or they will lose their shape.

5 Coat the rice balls in flour. Heat the vegetable oil in a large, heavy pan until a cube of bread, dropped in the oil, browns in 45 seconds. Deep-fry the rice balls, in batches, until crisp and golden. Lift out and drain on kitchen paper.

6 Put the rice balls into individual soup plates and ladle over the soup. Serve immediately.

SERVES 6

150g/5oz/⅔ cup long grain rice
50g/2oz Fontina cheese, grated
1 egg, beaten
30ml/2 tbsp freshly grated
  Parmesan cheese
15ml/1 tbsp olive oil
1.5 litres/2½ pints/6¼ cups meat
  stock, strained
1 large beetroot (beet), boiled
  for 1 hour, peeled and cut
  into matchsticks
1 large carrot, boiled for 20 minutes
  and cut into matchsticks
1 large yellow potato, peeled,
  boiled for 20 minutes and cut
  into matchsticks
1 large dark green courgette
  (zucchini), boiled briefly, then
  cut into matchsticks
60–90ml/4–6 tbsp plain
  (all-purpose) flour
vegetable oil, for deep-frying

PER PORTION Energy 415kcal/1726kJ; Protein 10.7g; Carbohydrate 36.9g, of which sugars 4.1g; Fat 25.1g, of which saturates 5.8g; Cholesterol 48mg; Calcium 197mg; Fibre 1.6g; Sodium 200mg.

200g/7oz pearl barley, rinsed
30–45ml/2–3 tbsp pork fat or
    olive oil
1 large onion, chopped
1 large carrot, chopped
1 or 2 celery sticks, chopped
handful of fresh flat leaf parsley,
    leaves chopped
4 fresh sage leaves, chopped
1 fresh rosemary sprig,
    leaves chopped
4 fresh marjoram sprigs,
    leaves chopped
30ml/2 tbsp plain (all-purpose) flour
2.25 litres/4 pints/10 cups
    meat stock
2 potatoes, peeled and chopped
1 meaty speck bone, or smoked
    ham bone
sea salt and ground black pepper
freshly grated Parmesan cheese,
    to serve

PER PORTION Energy 229kcal/969kJ; Protein 4.8g;
Carbohydrate 45.1g, of which sugars 4.5g; Fat 4.6g,
of which saturates 0.6g; Cholesterol 0mg;
Calcium 33mg; Fibre 1.6g; Sodium 9mg.

TRENTINO BARLEY SOUP
MINESTRA D'ORZO ALLA TRENTINA

This thick and creamy soup has lots of flavour with the added bonus of a meaty ham bone to make it really tasty and even more filling. The meat should fall off the bone and become a part of the soup as it cooks. This is a traditional and old-fashioned soup in Trentino, where barley is used in all kinds of different dishes. A similar soup can be made using beans or lentils instead of barley. Pork fat is the most common cooking fat used in the region, where olive oil is not produced.

1 Put the barley in a large pan and cover with plenty of water. Boil gently for 50 minutes, or until tender. Drain.

2 Put the pork fat or oil in a large pan and add the onion, carrot and celery, and most of the herbs. Set aside the remaining herbs for the garnish. Fry the vegetables and herbs gently until sizzling, then stir in the flour.

3 Add the drained barley, the stock, potatoes and seasoning. Stir, then add the speck or ham bone and submerge it in the liquid. Cover and simmer, stirring occasionally, for 1 hour, or until the meat has fallen off the bone and the vegetables are very soft.

4 Serve hot, garnished with the reserved herbs, with Parmesan cheese offered separately.

SERVES 4

300g/11oz/1¾ cup dried beans,
    preferably Lamon or borlotti,
    soaked overnight in cold water
    (alternatively, use 3 x 400g/
    14oz canned beans)
50ml/2fl oz/¼ cup olive oil or
    50g/2oz pork fat
75g/3oz fatty pancetta
1 onion, chopped
1 carrot, chopped
1 celery stick, chopped
1 litre/1¾ pints/4 cups good
    meat stock
150g/5oz tiny pasta (rice-grain size)
sea salt and ground black pepper

VENETIAN BEAN AND PASTA SOUP
PASTA E FAGIOLI

Every region of Italy has a version of this old recipe containing the cheapest of ingredients: a handful of pasta, a few vegetables, a little fatty pork, beans and stock. It varies from one place to another, but is very much representative of the peasant style of cooking in the Veneto, which contrasts sharply with the elegant dishes of the aristocracy. Just as Tuscany favours the borlotto bean, the Veneto too has its favourite variety for this dish, the Lamon bean, which may be hard to find outside of the region.

1 Drain the beans, put them into a large pan and cover with plenty of water. Boil rapidly for 5 minutes, then reduce the heat and simmer for 1 hour, or until tender. Drain.

2 Heat the olive oil or pork fat in a large pan and add the pancetta, onion, carrot and celery. Gently fry together over a medium heat for 5–10 minutes, until the vegetables are soft.

3 Add the beans and stir thoroughly. Add the stock and simmer slowly for 45–50 minutes, or until the beans are almost falling apart.

4 Add the pasta and cook for a further 10 minutes, or until the pasta is tender.

5 Season the soup to taste with salt and ground black pepper, and serve warm.

PER PORTION Energy 456kcal/1920kJ; Protein 24.7g; Carbohydrate 59.9g, of which sugars 6.7g; Fat 14.8g, of which saturates 2.9g; Cholesterol 12mg; Calcium 122mg; Fibre 12.9g; Sodium 267mg.

THE JOTA OF TRIESTE
LA JOTA TRIESTINA

This tremendously sustaining, rib-sticking soup is the pride of the city of Trieste and exists in various versions, although the basic principle of beans and cabbage remains the same. La Jota must be very thick once cooked and is generally thought to be much more delicious the day after it has been made, left to rest overnight and then gently reheated. It is sometimes served as an accompaniment to local meat dishes rather than as an appetizer.

1 Drain the beans, then rinse them thoroughly and transfer to a pan with fresh water to cover. Bring to the boil and boil rapidly for 5 minutes, then drain and rinse again.

2 Heat half the oil or butter in a large pan and fry the garlic, pancetta and potatoes for 5 minutes. Add the beans. Stir together, then add 1 litre/1¾ pints/4 cups water and cover. Bring to the boil, then simmer gently, stirring occasionally, for 1½ hours, or until the beans are tender. Add more water if necessary.

3 Put the sauerkraut, cumin and bay leaf in a pan and cover with water. Bring to the boil. Cook until the water has almost evaporated.

4 Heat the remaining oil or butter in a large frying pan. Add the flour and cook it until it is nutty brown. Add the cooked sauerkraut to the frying pan and stir together, then add half the bean mixture.

5 Push the remaining half of the bean mixture through a food mill into the soup. Alternatively, if you do not have a food mill, you could process the remaining half of the bean mixture in a food processor or blender, then add it to the soup.

6 Stir the soup well and season to taste, then cover and simmer for a further 30 minutes before serving.

SERVES 6

675g/1½lb/3¾ cups dried borlotti
  beans, soaked overnight in
  cold water (alternatively, use
  6 x 400g/14oz canned beans)
90ml/6 tbsp olive oil or 50g/2oz/
  ¼ cup unsalted butter
2 garlic cloves, chopped
115g/4oz smoked pancetta, cubed
3 potatoes, peeled and cubed
400g/14oz sauerkraut
5ml/1 tsp ground cumin
1 bay leaf
25ml/1½ tbsp plain (all-purpose) flour
sea salt and ground black pepper

PER PORTION Energy 504kcal/2123kJ; Protein 29.8g;
Carbohydrate 61.1g, of which sugars 4.4g; Fat 17.3g,
of which saturates 3.4g; Cholesterol 12mg;
Calcium 151mg; Fibre 19.8g; Sodium 663mg.

GRILLED POLENTA WITH MUSHROOMS
CROSTINI DI POLENTA CON FUNGHI

This is a quick and easy way to use up leftover polenta. It is a deliciously different appetizer that is filling and pretty to look at. You can vary the flavour by using fried onions instead of the mushrooms if you prefer, or make it really Venetian by adding some warm, braised radicchio leaves. Asiago is a local cheese of the Veneto and is much prized on the cheese board as well as in cooking.

1 Heat the grill (broiler) and lightly oil the polenta squares. Put the cheese in a heatproof bowl and add milk to cover. Set it over a pan of simmering water and allow the cheese to melt and blend with the milk, stirring frequently.

2 Meanwhile, put the remaining oil in a frying pan over a medium heat and fry the mushrooms and garlic, stirring frequently, for 10 minutes, until the mushrooms are cooked. Season.

3 When the cheese and milk have formed a smooth sauce, grill (broil) the polenta on both sides.

4 Arrange two squares of grilled polenta on each plate and cover with a spoonful of the melted cheese. Spoon the mushrooms evenly over the top, then sprinkle each portion with chopped flat leaf parsley and serve immediately.

SERVES 4

1 quantity Basic Polenta, cut into
  8 squares (see page 46)
45ml/3 tbsp olive oil
250g/9oz Asiago or Fontina
  cheese, cubed
a little milk
400g/14oz/5½ cups mushrooms, sliced
2 garlic cloves, thinly sliced
45ml/3 tbsp finely chopped fresh
  flat leaf parsley, to garnish
sea salt and ground black pepper

> **COOK'S TIP**
>
> To make braised radicchio leaves to accompany the polenta, put shredded radicchio leaves and a little butter in a pan, then cook gently until soft, adding a little water as needed.

PER PORTION Energy 518kcal/2155kJ; Protein 18.9g; Carbohydrate 46.2g, of which sugars 0.3g; Fat 27.2g, of which saturates 16.1g; Cholesterol 69mg; Calcium 334mg; Fibre 2.5g; Sodium 397mg.

SERVES 4

100g/3¾oz sultanas (golden raisins)
675g/1½lb fresh sardines, cleaned
   and heads removed
about 60ml/4 tbsp plain
   (all-purpose) flour
1 litre/1¾ pints/4 cups sunflower oil,
   for deep-frying
675g/1½lb white onions,
   thinly sliced
30ml/2 tbsp red wine vinegar
115g/4oz/¾ cup pine nuts
sea salt and ground black pepper

COOK'S TIP

If you are preparing the
sardines yourself, do be sure
to remove the central bone
carefully and gently so that
you do not destroy the shape
of the fish.

PER PORTION Energy 729kcal/3037kJ; Protein 41.5g;
Carbohydrate 31.8g, of which sugars 27.9g;
Fat 49.4g, of which saturates 7.5g; Cholesterol 0mg;
Calcium 203mg; Fibre 3.4g; Sodium 213mg.

SWEET-AND-SOUR FRIED SARDINES
SARDE IN SAOR

Sardines served this way make a traditional Venetian dish, and although the
ingredients sound quite unusual, the final combination is delicious. You will find this
on sale all over Venice, as it is extremely popular with the locals and there are lots
of variations on the basic theme. Ideally, you should leave the dish to rest in the
refrigerator for about 48 hours before eating it. Most important, however, is that
the sardines are fat and meaty, and as fresh as possible.

1 Soak the sultanas in warm water to cover for
20 minutes, or until plump. Meanwhile, wash
and dry the cleaned sardines carefully, then
toss them in flour to coat them all over.

2 Heat the oil in a large, heavy pan to
180°C/350°F, or until a small cube of bread
dropped into the oil browns in 40 seconds.
Fry the sardines until golden brown, then lift
out with a slotted spoon and drain them
thoroughly on kitchen paper. Leave to cool.

3 Carefully transfer 15ml/1 tbsp of the oil to a
separate pan, and fry the onions until just
golden. Add the vinegar and cook for 3 minutes
more. Season and remove from the heat.

4 Drain the sultanas. Arrange the ingredients
in layers in a serving dish as follows: a layer of
fish, then onions, then sultanas and pine nuts,
and so on, until all the ingredients have been
used up. Leave the dish to chill for 24–48 hours,
before serving.

SERVES 6

1kg/2¼lb salt cod, soaked for
   4 days with the water
   changed regularly
about 300ml/½ pint/1¼ cups
   extra virgin olive oil
60ml/4 tbsp finely chopped fresh
   flat leaf parsley, plus extra
   to garnish
2–4 garlic cloves, crushed
sea salt and ground black pepper
grilled (broiled) polenta, to serve

WHIPPED SALT COD IN THE VENETIAN STYLE
BACCALÀ MANTECATO ALLA VENEZIANA

Baccalà is dried salted cod, which needs four days of soaking in fresh cold water to reconstitute it, changing the water two or three times each day. This is not an easy dish to make, but you may have eaten it at one of the many bars and street-food outlets in Venice, and wondered how it was made. Should you have difficulty in getting the fish going, you can put it in a bowl over a pan of simmering water and mash it with a fork to soften it enough to help you work with it. You could also make it using a food processor, but you will not achieve the same kind of lightness.

1 Rinse the soaked fish carefully, then put it in a large pan and cover with fresh water. Bring to the boil and skim off any scum. Boil for 15–20 minutes, or until tender (you may need to cook it for a little longer if it is still tough).

2 Drain and cool. Once cold enough to handle, remove the skin and bones.

3 Transfer the fish to a large bowl and break into flakes.

4 'Whip' the fish with a large wooden spoon, gradually adding extra virgin olive oil in a fine, steady stream. Stop whipping when the fish is like whipped cream: white, and light and fluffy. The quantity of oil will depend upon the greasiness of the fish and how good the oil is.

5 Stir in the chopped parsley, garlic and pepper. Taste and add a little salt if necessary. Serve chilled, sprinkled with parsley and accompanied by grilled polenta.

PER PORTION Energy 435kcal/1803kJ; Protein 30.7g; Carbohydrate 0.2g, of which sugars 0.2g; Fat 34.6g, of which saturates 4.8g; Cholesterol 77mg; Calcium 28mg; Fibre 0.3g; Sodium 102mg.

GRILLED MIXED SEAFOOD
FRUTTI DI MARE GRATINATI

A lovely, simple antipasto, this grilled dish makes the most of the delicious selection of seafood available from the fish markets of Venice, but it can be made anywhere. As with any seafood dish, it is the freshness of the raw material that makes all the difference. It is far better to reduce the number of shellfish varieties to one or two and eat them absolutely fresh, than to have lots of different varieties that may not be at their very best.

1 Scrub the mussels with a stiff brush and rinse under cold running water. Discard any that remain open after being sharply tapped. Scrape off any barnacles and remove the 'beards' with a small knife. Rinse well. Scrub the oysters, scallops and clams with a stiff brush to remove any sand. Gently scrub the razor shells.

2 Put the shellfish into a large pan – you do not need to add any water. Steam them for 5–8 minutes over a medium heat, or until the shells open. Immediately, remove the pan from the heat and lift out the shellfish. Discard any that remain closed.

3 Preheat the grill (broiler) to high. Remove one half of each shell and put all the shellfish in their half-shells into a wide, ovenproof dish or on a baking sheet.

4 Mix together the breadcrumbs, Parmesan cheese, garlic, parsley and seasoning. Cover the top of each shellfish with this mixture, then drizzle generously with the oil.

5 Put the dish or baking sheet under the grill for 5 minutes to brown, then serve immediately either on individual plates or a large serving platter.

SERVES 4

16 mussels
8 oysters
4 scallops
20 large Venus clams
4 razor shells
60ml/4 tbsp fresh breadcrumbs
60ml/4 tbsp freshly grated
   Parmesan cheese
3 garlic cloves, finely chopped
45ml/3 tbsp chopped fresh parsley
75ml/5 tbsp olive oil
sea salt and ground black pepper

PER PORTION Energy 367kcal/1530kJ; Protein 23.9g; Carbohydrate 16.8g, of which sugars 4.4g; Fat 23.1g, of which saturates 5.9g; Cholesterol 184mg; Calcium 299mg; Fibre 2.5g; Sodium 516mg.

BREAD DUMPLINGS
CANEDERLI

In Trentino-Alto Adige these simple bread dumplings, floating in a meaty broth, are served as an antipasto, before a main course of meat with polenta. As with many recipes from this region, the cheapest of ingredients are turned into nourishing food. Brown bread is common in these parts, so it is likely that the breadcrumbs used would be wholemeal (whole-wheat). Many different versions of canederli exist, some with the addition of chopped bacon, or pork fat instead of butter.

1 Crumble or grate the bread finely. Transfer the crumbs to a mixing bowl and add the butter. Mix well.

2 Add the eggs, parsley, flour and nutmeg, and mix well. Season with salt. Stir in the warmed milk to make a fairly soft paste.

3 Leave to stand for 30 minutes to allow the bread to swell. Dampen your hands and shape the mixture into balls 5cm/2in in diameter.

4 Bring the stock to a gentle boil in a pan and add the balls. Simmer for 20 minutes, then serve sprinkled with extra parsley.

SERVES 4

350g/12oz dried bread
100g/3¾oz unsalted butter, softened
4 eggs, beaten
60ml/4 tbsp finely chopped fresh
   flat leaf parsley, plus extra
   to garnish
115g/4oz/1 cup plain (all-purpose)
   or wholemeal (whole-wheat) flour
1.5ml/¼ tsp freshly grated nutmeg
200ml/7fl oz/scant 1 cup full cream
   (whole) milk, warmed
1.5 litres/2½ pints/6¼ cups rich
   meat stock
sea salt

PER PORTION Energy 584kcal/2447kJ; Protein 18.5g; Carbohydrate 63.9g, of which sugars 5.8g; Fat 30.2g, of which saturates 16.7g; Cholesterol 255mg; Calcium 243mg; Fibre 4.6g; Sodium 763mg.

300ml/½ pint/1¼ cups full cream
(whole) milk
25g/1oz fresh yeast
200g/7oz/2 cups porridge oats
10ml/2 tsp cumin seeds
400g/14oz wholemeal
(whole-wheat) flour
vegetable oil, for greasing
sea salt

PER ROLL Energy 378kcal/1602kJ; Protein 14.5g; Carbohydrate 69.9g, of which sugars 3.8g; Fat 6.5g, of which saturates 1.4g; Cholesterol 7mg; Calcium 104mg; Fibre 8.3g; Sodium 41mg.

WHOLEMEAL AND OAT ROLLS
FILONCINI ALL'AVENA

These rolls, which are from Trentino-Alto Adige, use cumin, the most typical and memorable flavour of the north-east of the country. Cumin is used to make everything from liqueurs to desserts and is also added to stews and soups. Served warm with plenty of unsalted butter, these rolls are delicious with a bowl of hearty bean soup or dipped into frothy hot chocolate on a cold winter's day. Alternatively, split them open, top with cheese and toast them until it melts.

1 Warm the milk until tepid and then put into a bowl and mix in the yeast. Leave to stand until frothy.

2 In a mortar crush the oats and cumin seeds using a pestle. Transfer the mixture to a large bowl and add a pinch of salt and the flour.

3 Turn this out on to the work surface and make a hollow in the centre with your fist. Gently pour the yeast and milk into the hollow, then begin to mix everything together with your hands. Use stronger pressure once you have achieved a ball of dough.

4 Knead for 15 minutes, then transfer to a floured bowl and cover with a floured cloth. Leave for 3 hours, or until doubled in volume.

5 Punch down (knock back) the dough, then divide evenly into six balls. Lay them on a lightly oiled baking sheet, then leave to rise in a warm place for 2 hours, or until doubled in size.

6 Preheat the oven to 200°C/400°F/Gas 6. Snip the balls twice on the top and bake for 20 minutes until light golden brown; they should sound hollow when tapped underneath. Cool on a wire rack.

PASTA, GNOCCHI, RICE AND POLENTA
PASTA, GNOCCHI, RISO E POLENTA

Traditionally, pasta does not form part of the cuisine in this part of Italy, although the ubiquitous, soup-like pasta e fagioli is relied upon as a staple in both winter and summer. Although some pasta dishes have been imported from elsewhere and are now enjoyed in this region, this is the one area of Italy where pasta does not hold the primary position on the primi menu. Much more relevant to the north-east are creamy, almost soupy, risottos, and of course the most typical dish of them all, polenta, which is served with any variety of accompaniments including snails, frog's legs, beans, cheese, butter and baccalà. Sometimes white and sometimes yellow, sometimes coarsely ground and sometimes extremely fine, the great pot of bubbling maize meal porridge is ever present; and once enough of the freshly cooked version has been consumed, the cooled remainder will be sliced, then fried or grilled.

DUMPLINGS, POLENTA AND SOUPY RISOTTO

It doesn't take a visitor to this region long to discover that the menu here is not peppered with the classic Italian favourites, such as pasta with tomato sauce or spaghetti Bolognese. The food of the north-east of Italy is far removed from the cuisine of the south, and even the rest of northern Italy. It is hard to believe that one is still in the same country at times; this is a world away from the land of pizza, pasta and ice cream.

Risotto and polenta vie for position at this crucial point of the menu, the primo, which, for all Italians, is the most important phase of the whole meal – a full Italian meal would consist of an appetizer, followed by a primo, then a meat or fish course, and finally a dessert. Risotto is often served as a primo, followed by a light meat or fish dish. The further east one travels, the wetter and sloppier the risotto tends to become. A typical example of this is the Venetian Rice and Peas, which is hovering right on the edge of being a soup.

Polenta, on the other hand, is high in carbohydrate and makes you feel quite full initially, but is digested very quickly so you are soon hungry again. For this reason, it is usually served with a generous helping of meat, fish or cheese. This makes it more palatable, and combines two courses into one.

Gnocchi also deserve a mention, as they are wonderfully satisfying, making them perfect cold-weather food. The Italian version of the much-loved Austrian dumplings, they are frequently found here. They can be made out of many ingredients, including bread, potato, beetroot, or even polenta, and they are a perfect restorative after a winter's walk around the canals and churches of Venice.

GIANT BEETROOT AND MASCARPONE RAVIOLI
RAVIOLONI ROSA

This dish always looks so beautiful with the brilliant heliotrope pink of the beetroot against the white of the pasta, sitting in a little pool of melted butter studded with poppy seeds. This unusual pasta dish comes from the Trieste area, and really does taste as good as it looks. Make sure the pasta isn't too thin, so that the beetroot filling doesn't bleed through too much, as it would spoil the surprise of cutting the ravioli open once it is on the plate.

1 To make the filling, cook the beetroot in a large pan of water for 1 hour. Then remove from the heat and leave it to cool in the water until just warm. Drain, peel and cut into cubes. Process or blend until smooth.

2 Add the mascarpone to the beetroot to make a smooth, fairly thick purée. Stir in the Parmesan cheese and the cumin, then season to taste with salt and pepper. Chill until required.

3 Pile the flour in a mound on the work top, make a hollow in the centre and pour the eggs into it.

4 Mix the eggs into the flour with your fingertips, then knead the dough with both hands for at least 10 minutes, gradually adding the oil as you work.

5 Roll out the dough thinly. (If you have a pasta machine, roll it out to the penultimate thickness.)

6 Cut the rolled-out dough into eight sheets approximately 10cm/4in wide and 24cm/9½in long. Drop four 15ml/1 tbsp heaps of filling evenly spaced along four of the sheets, leaving even gaps all the way around the filling.

7 Lay the remaining four sheets on top and, with a pastry wheel, cut each strip into four across the width, then trim around the edges, well away from the filling. Make sure you seal all the edges very thoroughly as you cut. This will make a total of four ravioli per sheet, for a total of 16 ravioli; four per portion.

8 For the dressing, melt the butter in a small pan until liquid and nutty brown. Remove from the heat, stir in the poppy seeds and leave to stand for 15 minutes. Meanwhile, bring a large pan of salted water to the boil.

9 Slide the ravioli into the gently boiling water and cook for 4–5 minutes, or until they float on the surface and the pasta is just tender. Scoop out with a slotted spoon and arrange four ravioli on each of four warmed plates. Spoon over the warm poppy seed butter. Serve immediately, with Parmesan offered separately.

PER PORTION Energy 759kcal/3179kJ; Protein 23.5g; Carbohydrate 84.6g, of which sugars 7.9g; Fat 38.8g, of which saturates 22.4g; Cholesterol 280mg; Calcium 278mg; Fibre 4.5g; Sodium 422mg.

SERVES 4

400g/14oz/3½ cups plain
  (all-purpose) flour
4 large (US extra large) eggs, beaten
2.5ml/½ tsp extra virgin olive oil
sea salt

FOR THE FILLING
2 large beetroot (beets)
150g/5oz/⅔ cup mascarpone
30ml/2 tbsp freshly grated
  Parmesan cheese, plus extra
  to serve
large pinch of ground cumin
sea salt and ground black pepper

FOR THE DRESSING
115g/4oz/½ cup unsalted butter
7.5ml/1½ tsp poppy seeds

COOK'S TIPS

• It is important to use raw and not pickled beetroot for this recipe, because the vinegary flavour would completely overpower everything else.
• If you prefer, you can cook the ravioli in a light stock.

PAPARELE WITH CHICKEN LIVERS
PAPARELE E FIGADINI

Pastasciutta is the Italian word that refers to a dish of pasta that is drained, tossed with a sauce and served dry apart from the sauce. An alternative first course is a soup in which pasta has been cooked – this is a minestra or zuppa with pasta. This particular Venetian speciality is a cross between the two, and it relies heavily on the freshness and good quality of the chicken livers, and the dense richness of the stock. Although the pasta is called paparele, which is probably the dialect for pappardelle, these thumb-wide strips are not the same as the wide ribbons that are Tuscany's most traditional pasta shape. Unusually, the dough contains a little milk to make it even softer and more fragile.

1 Put the flour on to the work surface and make a hollow in the centre with your fist. Beat the eggs and milk together and pour into the hollow. Using your fingertips, bring the flour and liquid together, then knead until you have achieved a smooth, elastic ball of dough.

2 Roll out the dough thinly. Cut into 2cm/¾in strips with a sharp knife and leave to dry on a floured surface for about 30 minutes.

3 To cook the livers, heat the butter in a large pan and fry the chicken livers for 3–5 minutes, or until well browned. Add the beef stock.

4 Bring to the boil and add the pasta. Cook for 5 minutes, or until the pasta is al dente, then stir in the Parmesan cheese.

5 Sprinkle with the chopped parsley and serve with extra Parmesan on top.

SERVES 4

300g/11oz/2¾ cups plain (all-purpose) flour, plus extra for dusting
3 eggs
30ml/2 tbsp milk

FOR THE CHICKEN LIVERS

50g/2oz/¼ cup unsalted butter
175g/6oz chicken livers, washed and trimmed
1 litre/1¾ pints/4 cups beef stock
50g/2oz/⅔ cup freshly grated Parmesan cheese, plus extra to garnish
sea salt
chopped fresh parsley, to garnish

PER PORTION Energy 526kcal/2211kJ; Protein 25.7g; Carbohydrate 59.3g, of which sugars 1.8g; Fat 20.7g, of which saturates 11.6g; Cholesterol 351mg; Calcium 316mg; Fibre 3g; Sodium 330mg.

2 raw beetroot (beets)
2 eggs, beaten
200g/7oz/1¾ cups wholemeal
   (whole-wheat) flour
45ml/3 tbsp sunflower oil
1.5ml/¼ tsp freshly grated nutmeg
sea salt
40g/1½oz/3 tbsp unsalted butter,
   cubed, plus extra for greasing
60ml/4 tbsp freshly grated
   Parmesan cheese

PER PORTION Energy 423kcal/1771kJ; Protein 15.7g;
Carbohydrate 37.7g, of which sugars 6.3g; Fat 24.5g,
of which saturates 9.9g; Cholesterol 131mg;
Calcium 200mg; Fibre 5.9g; Sodium 297mg.

BEETROOT DUMPLINGS
SPAETZLE

This is a traditional dish from the remote mountainous region of Trentino-Alto Adige where beetroot is used in many recipes. Locally, you can buy a special instrument for cutting the spaetzle dough to the correct shape and size, but a wide-holed ricer works reasonably well. Failing this, use two teaspoons to form small dumplings that can be neatly dropped into the water. This recipe is from the northern part of the region, close to the Austrian border, where most people still speak German.

1 Put the beetroot in a large pan of water, bring to the boil and cook for 45 minutes, or until tender. Leave to cool in the water, then drain, reserving the water. Peel the beetroot.

2 Push the cooked beetroot through a food mill into a mixing bowl to make a smooth purée. Add the eggs, 150ml/¼ pint/⅔ cup of the reserved beetroot water, the flour, oil and nutmeg. Season with salt and leave to rest for about 20 minutes. Preheat the oven to 180°C/350°F/Gas 4.

3 Bring a wide pan of salted water to the boil and press the mixture into the boiling water through a wide-holed ricer, or use two teaspoons to form small dumplings and drop them into the water. As soon as the dumplings rise to the surface of the water, scoop them out with a slotted spoon and arrange them in a buttered ovenproof dish.

4 Sprinkle with the butter cubes and the Parmesan cheese, then bake for 20 minutes, or until golden. Serve hot.

GNOCCHI IN THE STYLE OF VICENZA
GNOCCHI ALLA VICENTINA

This dish is intended to be a first course, or primo, despite being sweet. The sweetness comes from the sugar mixed into the cinnamon, as well as the sultanas soaked in fiery grappa. Grappa is a much-loved drink in all these regions and is a wonderful way to keep out the cold. Made from the grape residue left after the wine has been pressed, it is a clear spirit that is about 40 per cent proof. It is used in various local dishes, and is also added to espresso coffee to make a potent caffè corretto.

1 Boil the potatoes until soft, then drain and peel them. Press the cooked potatoes through a potato ricer twice or mash them finely.

2 Blend half of the beaten eggs into the potato, then gradually add the flour, mixing with a spoon. Add as little flour and egg as possible for the gnocchi to hold their shape without disintegrating. Too much egg or flour will make the gnocchi heavy and rubbery. To test if the texture is right, roughly shape two or three gnocchi and drop them into a small pan of simmering salted water. If they float up to the surface within a minute, and have a light texture when you bite into them, then the dough is ready and you can shape the rest.

3 Using your hands, work carefully and quickly to shape the gnocchi – the more you handle the dough, the harder it will become. Roll the soft dough into long, thumb-thick cylinders. Cut into sections of about 2.5cm/1in, and form into small concave gnocchi shapes, by pressing them against the back of a fork.

4 Spread out the gnocchi on a large floured board and set aside until required.

5 Soak the sultanas in the grappa and gently melt the butter in a small pan over a low heat. Mix together the sugar and cinnamon and set aside.

6 Bring a large pan of salted water to the boil, drop in the gnocchi in batches and allow them to cook for about 1 minute until they float on the surface. Remove them with a slotted spoon and arrange in a well-buttered ovenproof dish. (You will need about 12 gnocchi per person.)

7 Sprinkle the gnocchi with the soaked sultanas, then drizzle over the melted butter and any of the soaking grappa that is left in the bowl. Sprinkle over the sugar and cinnamon mixture and place the dressed gnocchi in a low oven to keep warm while you boil the remaining gnocchi and dress them in the same way.

8 Once all the gnocchi are dressed, serve immediately.

SERVES 6

1kg/2¼lb floury potatoes, unpeeled
3 eggs, beaten
250g/9oz/2¼ cups plain
   (all-purpose) flour
50g/2oz sultanas (golden raisins)
45ml/3 tbsp grappa
200g/7oz/scant 1 cup unsalted
   butter, plus extra for greasing
50g/2oz/¼ cup sugar
25g/1oz/2 tbsp ground cinnamon
sea salt

VARIATION

For a more savoury flavour, you could serve the cooked gnocchi simply drizzled with melted butter and sprinkled with some freshly grated Parmesan cheese.

PER PORTION Energy 379kcal/1607kJ; Protein 10.8g; Carbohydrate 75.2g, of which sugars 17.3g; Fat 4.4g, of which saturates 1.1g; Cholesterol 95mg; Calcium 100mg; Fibre 3.1g; Sodium 58mg.

BASIC POLENTA
LA POLENTA

Polenta is the basic staple starch eaten all over the north of Italy. Made from ground maize, it can be white or yellow, and comes in various different grades: fine, medium or coarse. The widely-available quick-cook variety is frowned upon by purists who claim that only the real thing, which requires up to an hour of constant stirring, will have the correct flavour. Serve in a slab with a slice of Gorgonzola on top, which melts over the hot polenta, or alongside a stew. It can also be served soft in a bowl with a stew, dressing, sauce or cheese on the top.

1 Put the water into a wide, heavy pan over a high heat and bring back to the boil. Add a large pinch of salt.

2 Trickle the polenta flour into the boiling water in a fine rain with one hand, while whisking constantly with the other.

3 When all the polenta flour has been whisked into the water, reduce the heat to medium-low.

4 Stir with a strong, long-handled wooden spoon until the polenta comes away from the sides of the pan. This will take 40–50 minutes.

5 Turn the polenta out on to a board and smooth it into a mound shape using spatulas. Leave it to rest for about 5 minutes.

6 Cut the polenta into six thick slabs. Distribute the Gorgonzola evenly over each portion. Serve immediately, while still hot.

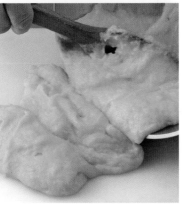

SERVES 6

1.75 litres/3 pints/7½ cups
  boiling water
200–225g/7–8oz/scant 2 cups
  polenta flour
200g/7oz Gorgonzola, sliced
sea salt

PER PORTION Energy 238kcal/992kJ; Protein 9.8g; Carbohydrate 24.4g, of which sugars 0g; Fat 11g, of which saturates 6.2g; Cholesterol 25mg; Calcium 168mg; Fibre 0.7g; Sodium 420mg.

300ml/½ pint/1¼ cups boiling water

300ml/½ pint/1¼ cups full cream (whole) milk

350g/12oz/3 cups medium-grade polenta flour

115g/4oz/½ cup unsalted butter

115g/4oz/1 cup grated Asiago cheese, or another cheese

150g/5oz/⅔ cup ricotta cheese

sea salt

PER PORTION Energy 770kcal/3200kJ; Protein 21.5g; Carbohydrate 68.8g, of which sugars 4.8g; Fat 44.2g, of which saturates 27g; Cholesterol 120mg; Calcium 306mg; Fibre 1.9g; Sodium 465mg.

DRESSED POLENTA
POLENTA CONZATA

Soft polenta is particularly tasty served this simple way. You can use any strong-tasting cheese to flavour the hot polenta, but in the Veneto they would use their local cheese, which is called Asiago. As polenta is relatively bland in taste, it can take on all kinds of different flavours. Make sure you keep the consistency quite soft, as it is served in shallow bowls and eaten with a spoon. You can use white or yellow polenta in this recipe – it is a matter of personal preference.

1 Put the water and milk into a large, heavy pan over high heat and bring to the boil. Add a good pinch of salt.

2 Trickle the polenta flour into the boiling liquid in a fine rain with one hand, while whisking constantly with the other.

3 When all the polenta flour has been whisked in, reduce the heat to medium-low.

4 Stir with a strong, long-handled wooden spoon until the polenta comes away from the sides of the pan, but is not stiff. This will take 40–50 minutes.

5 Melt the butter and stir it through the polenta.

6 Divide the grated cheese and ricotta among four bowls, pour the buttered polenta on top and serve immediately.

POLENTA WITH TOMATOES
POLENTA CON POMODORI

SERVES 4

4 large ripe tomatoes, sliced
750ml/1¼ pints/3 cups boiling water
200g/7oz/1¾ cups medium-grade
   white polenta flour
45ml/3 tbsp extra virgin olive oil
1 fresh thyme sprig, leaves chopped
1 fresh marjoram sprig,
   leaves chopped
50g/2oz freshly grated
   Pecorino cheese
sea salt and ground black pepper
vegetable oil, for greasing

This is a relatively modern way of preparing polenta and is a recipe from Friuli-Venezia Giulia. In this region, white polenta is preferred to the yellow variety, as it is considered to have a much more delicate flavour, best suited to the local dishes. Although tomatoes and olive oil are not a major part of the cuisine of this area, they all work well together in this dish. It makes a very tasty lunch or supper, to which other ingredients, such as sliced salami, could be added.

1 Sprinkle the tomatoes with salt and lay them in a colander to drain for about 30 minutes. Preheat the oven to 200°C/400°F/Gas 6 and cover a baking sheet with baking parchment.

2 Drain the tomatoes and lay them on the prepared baking parchment. Bake in the hot oven for 4 minutes.

3 Put the water into a wide, heavy pan over a high heat and return to the boil. Add a good pinch of salt, then trickle the polenta flour into the boiling water in a fine rain with one hand, while whisking constantly with the other.

4 When all the polenta flour has been whisked into the water, reduce the heat to medium-low and stir with a strong, long-handled wooden spoon until the polenta comes away from the sides of the pan. This will take 40–50 minutes.

5 Remove from the heat and stir in 30ml/2 tbsp olive oil. Spread it evenly into a greased 20 x 30cm/8 x 12in ovenproof dish.

6 Arrange the tomato slices on top and sprinkle with the chopped herbs, the Pecorino cheese and the remaining olive oil. Bake for 10 minutes, or until the cheese has browned. Serve.

PER PORTION Energy 336kcal/1401kJ; Protein 10.7g; Carbohydrate 40g, of which sugars 3.4g; Fat 14.5g, of which saturates 3.8g; Cholesterol 13mg; Calcium 184mg; Fibre 2.7g; Sodium 150mg.

BEAN AND RAISIN POLENTA
MANAI

Polenta cooked with pork stock and bacon reflects the basic cuisine of the region with a touch of sophistication added by plump, sweet raisins. The variety of beans best loved by the Venetians is called Lamon and is considered by connoisseurs to be more tasty than the more common borlotti type. The polenta flour needs to be coarsely ground to give the dish the correct texture. If you prefer, you can leave out the raisins, although traditionally they would have been a crucial feature of the dish.

1 Put the raisins in a small bowl and cover with hot water. Leave to soak until plump, then drain and pat dry with kitchen paper. Set aside.

2 Put the beans into a large pan with enough water to cover, and boil hard for 5 minutes. Drain and rinse.

3 Put the stock in the pan and add the pork bones and beans. Bring to the boil and simmer for 45 minutes, or until the beans are soft.

4 Chop the bacon. Remove the bones, add the onion, bacon and raisins, and stir.

5 Bring the stock back to the boil.

6 Trickle the polenta flour into the boiling stock in a fine rain with one hand, while whisking constantly with the other.

7 When all the polenta flour has been whisked into the stock, reduce the heat to medium-low. Stir with a strong, long-handled wooden spoon until the polenta comes away from the sides of the pan. This will take about 45 minutes.

8 Season with salt and serve piping hot.

SERVES 4

45ml/3 tbsp raisins
200g/7oz/generous 1 cup dried
    Lamon or borlotti beans, soaked
    overnight and drained
3 litres/5¼ pints/12 cups light
    pork stock
1kg/2¼lb raw pork bones
115g/4oz streaky (fatty) bacon
1 large onion, peeled
300g/11oz/2¾ cups coarse yellow
    polenta flour
sea salt

PER PORTION Energy 555kcal/2330kJ; Protein 24.1g;
Carbohydrate 92.6g, of which sugars 14.7g;
Fat 10.2g, of which saturates 2.5g; Cholesterol 19mg;
Calcium 84mg; Fibre 11.1g; Sodium 381mg.

RISOTTO WITH TROUT
RISOTTO CON LE TROTE

Lovely and creamy, this trout risotto uses lots of spices to add a real Venetian twist to the dish. You could also use other kinds of fish, but the delicate flavour of trout works especially well. Make sure the trout is really fresh for the best results and that the spices have not lost any of their pungency. This is especially delicious if served with a chilled Soave, the Veneto's best-known white wine. As with all fish-based rice or pasta recipes, no cheese is offered with this dish.

SERVES 4

1 bay leaf
5 black peppercorns
½ cinnamon stick
2 cloves
pinch of freshly grated nutmeg
pinch of ground ginger
pinch of ground allspice
60ml/4 tbsp chopped fresh flat leaf
    parsley, plus 30ml/2 tbsp chopped
    fresh flat leaf parsley, to garnish
2 or 3 small fresh trout, about
    600g/1lb 5oz total weight,
    cleaned and gutted
75g/3oz/6 tbsp unsalted butter
30ml/2 tbsp olive oil
1 garlic clove, chopped
350g/12oz vialone nano rice
175ml/6fl oz/¾ cup dry white wine
sea salt

1 Put the bay leaf, spices and parsley into a pan large enough to take the fish, and cover with water. Simmer gently for 10 minutes, then lower the trout into the water.

2 Poach for 5 minutes, then cover and remove from the heat. Leave the trout in the hot water until cooked through. The cooking time needed will depend on the size of each fish.

3 Remove the trout, then skin and fillet them. Strain the stock into a pan. Bring to the boil then reduce the heat to a simmer.

4 Heat 40g/1½oz/3 tbsp butter and the oil in a heavy pan, add the garlic and cook until just softened. Add the rice and toast the grains well, then add the wine and cook for 2 minutes.

5 Add one ladleful of hot fish stock and cook, stirring constantly, until the liquid is absorbed. Continue in this way, adding the stock a ladleful at a time and stirring constantly. Always allow the liquid to be absorbed before adding more.

6 After the rice has been cooking for about 20 minutes, stir in the fish fillets, breaking them up as you stir them through.

7 When the rice is tender, remove the pan from the heat and stir in the remaining butter.

8 Cover and leave to rest for 2 minutes, then transfer to a platter. Sprinkle with the chopped parsley and serve immediately.

PER PORTION Energy 615kcal/2565kJ; Protein 29.9g; Carbohydrate 70.1g, of which sugars 0.3g; Fat 20.3g, of which saturates 11.2g; Cholesterol 139mg; Calcium 59mg; Fibre 0g; Sodium 229mg.

SERVES 4

2 litres/3½ pints/9 cups beef, veal,
    vegetable or chicken stock
1kg/2¼lb young fresh peas, in their
    pods, or 400g/14oz frozen petits
    pois (baby peas), thawed
60ml/4 tbsp extra virgin olive oil
50g/2oz/¼ cup unsalted butter
½ mild, sweet onion, finely chopped
50g/2oz pancetta, chopped
25g/1oz chopped fresh flat
    leaf parsley
300g/11oz short grain rice,
    preferably vialone nano gigante
100g/3¾oz/generous 1 cup freshly
    grated Parmesan cheese, plus
    extra to serve
sea salt and ground black pepper

VENETIAN RICE AND PEAS
RISI E BISI

This is a very typical Venetian recipe that is cooked in the old way of making risotto, without frying the rice in fat at the beginning. The end result is more like a very thick soup than a risotto. Not all recipes for rice and peas call for pancetta, but it adds flavour and is great in the chilly winter. The choice of rice variety is important, as the rice needs to become very soft while still keeping its shape. Bear in mind that this dish is served much wetter than other risottos, and should have a soupy texture.

1 Bring the stock to the boil in a large pan, then allow to simmer over a low-medium heat. If using peas in their pods, shell the peas and add the pods to the simmering stock.

2 Put the olive oil and butter in a heavy pan, add the onion and pancetta, and fry gently for 10 minutes, or until the onion is softened. Stir in the parsley. Fry gently for 4 minutes more. Add the peas and stir thoroughly.

3 Add enough stock to barely cover the vegetables. Simmer very slowly for 3–4 minutes until the peas are tender. Add the rice, stir and add a further two ladlefuls of stock.

4 Season and stir, then cook until the grains have almost completely absorbed the stock. Add another two ladlefuls of stock, keeping the mixture very moist.

5 Continue in this way, adding the stock two ladlefuls at a time and stirring constantly, until the rice is tender. Always allow the liquid to be absorbed before adding more.

6 When the rice is soft and tender, remove from the heat and stir in the cheese. Cover and leave to rest for 3 minutes, then distribute between shallow bowls to serve. Offer extra grated Parmesan to sprinkle on top.

PER PORTION Energy 729kcal/3028kJ; Protein 34.8g; Carbohydrate 89.3g, of which sugars 6.6g; Fat 26.3g, of which saturates 8.5g; Cholesterol 33mg; Calcium 371mg; Fibre 12g; Sodium 433mg.

RISOTTO OF THE SERENE REPUBLIC GUARDS
RISOTTO ALLA SBIRRAGLIA

This simple but rich chicken risotto is named after the men who guarded the treasures of Venice when it was known as La Serenissima, or the Serene Republic (the guards were called sbirraglia, or sbirri, and the latter term is still used as slang to refer to the police). The use of vialone rice reflects the importance that Italians place on their local ingredients. It is very hard grained and is the rice most traditionally used in this region. The larger type, gigante, is hard to find outside of Italy or indeed the region itself, but fortunately vialone nano is easier to find, as it is widely exported.

1 Heat half the butter in a large pan, add the onion and fry until pale golden. Add the chicken cubes and cook gently, stirring frequently, until lightly browned.

2 Pour in the wine and cook for 2 minutes to allow the alcohol to evaporate, then add the rice. Stir thoroughly, then add one ladleful of stock and cook, stirring constantly, until the liquid is absorbed.

3 Continue adding stock a ladleful at a time and stirring constantly, for about 25–30 minutes, until the rice is tender. Always allow the liquid to be absorbed before adding more.

4 Stir in the remaining butter and half the cheese. Add salt if needed, then remove from the heat. Cover and leave to rest for 3 minutes, then transfer to a platter. Sprinkle with black pepper and the remaining cheese, and serve.

SERVES 4

50g/2oz/¼ cup unsalted butter
½ onion, finely chopped
500g/1¼lb skinless chicken, cubed
175ml/6fl oz/¾ cup dry white wine
350g/12oz vialone nano gigante or
   vialone nano rice
1 litre/1¾ pints/4 cups rich beef
   stock, simmering
60ml/4 tbsp freshly grated
   Parmesan cheese
sea salt and ground black pepper

PER PORTION Energy 580kcal/2421kJ; Protein 39g; Carbohydrate 61g, of which sugars 0.9g; Fat 19.5g, of which saturates 11.1g; Cholesterol 98mg; Calcium 213mg; Fibre 0.2g; Sodium 348mg.

RICE AND SAUSAGES
RISO E LUGANEGA

The luganega sausage is made in a long coil, and different versions appear in various parts of the country. Two theories exist in these parts regarding the name: one is that it is somehow connected to the city of Lugana in Switzerland. The other, more likely, is that the name is derived from the word for 'long', which in Italian is lungo. However, just to confuse things further, there is also a regional sausage with the same name that is short and slim, and not made in a continuous coil! This is a Venetian risotto and should be served quite wet and soupy.

1 Peel and crumble two of the sausages, leaving the other two whole.

2 Heat 40g/1½oz/3 tbsp butter and the oil in a large pan, add the onion and fry, stirring, until just golden.

3 Add the crumbled sausages and fry, stirring frequently, until they are just cooked, but not browned.

4 Add the rice. Stir until well mixed. Add the wine and cook for 2 minutes to evaporate the alcohol.

5 Add two ladlefuls of stock. Stir constantly until the liquid has almost all been absorbed, then add another two ladlefuls of stock and stir as before.

6 Continue adding the stock two ladlefuls at a time and stirring constantly, for 10 minutes.

7 Add the two whole sausages, then continue to add stock and cook as before until the rice is tender. It will take about 25 minutes for the rice to cook.

8 When the rice is tender, check the seasoning, and add salt only if necessary. Stir in the rest of the butter and half the cheese. Remove from the heat. Cover and leave to rest for 3 minutes.

9 Remove the sausages and slice them. Transfer the risotto to a serving platter and top with the sausages. Sprinkle over the remaining cheese.

SERVES 4

4 x 18cm/7in lengths of
  luganega sausage
75g/3oz/6 tbsp unsalted butter
30ml/2 tbsp olive oil
½ white onion, finely chopped
350g/12oz arborio rice
175ml/6fl oz/¾ cup dry white wine
1 litre/1¾ pints/4 cups rich beef
  stock, simmering
75ml/5 tbsp freshly grated
  Parmesan cheese
sea salt

COOK'S TIP

All Venetian risottos are quite wet and liquid once cooked. If you run out of stock, use boiling water instead. Remember to allow all the liquid to be absorbed before adding more, and to keep the stock constantly simmering.

PER PORTION Energy 995kcal/4133kJ; Protein 26.2g; Carbohydrate 85.9g, of which sugars 3.4g; Fat 57.5g, of which saturates 27.3g; Cholesterol 112mg; Calcium 312mg; Fibre 0.8g; Sodium 1360mg.

FISH AND SHELLFISH
PESCE E FRUTTI DI MARE

One of the most important wholesale fish and shellfish markets of the whole of northern Italy is based at the port of Chioggia, in the province of Venice, and restaurateurs from as far away as Tuscany come and shop here before the sun rises in the very early hours of the morning. Every imaginable variety, size and shape of fish is available, but only for a short period of time as the market is extremely busy and sells out in a few hours. Soft-shelled crabs, spider crabs, scallops, squid, whiting and sole are widely-used ingredients, among other fish and shellfish, in the dishes of the region. Also hugely popular all over the north-east, as in many other areas of Italy, are baccalà (salt cod) and stoccafisso (dried cod), which are often stewed and served with polenta.

SALT COD, SOLE, SQUID AND SCALLOPS

....

People in the coastal areas of Veneto and Friuli-Venezia Giulia are extremely fond of fresh fish and shellfish, and they form the basis of many local recipes. The capitals of these regions, Venice and Trieste respectively, are home to fabulous markets and wonderful restaurants selling all kinds of fresh seafood.

In Venice you might seek out the Pescheria, the fish market, along the Grand Canal, not far from the Rialto Bridge. The building that houses the fish market is easy to recognize by the red blinds hanging between the columns of the arcades. The very first fish market that existed on this spot dates back to the 11th century. The neo-gothic style building you can see now was built in the same position in 1907.

In Friuli-Venezia Giulia, Trieste is dotted with countless restaurants, to suit all pockets, serving fish and shellfish in all shapes and sizes. Sardoni, outsize sardines, are the most popular fish here, and they are normally served fried, in breadcrumbs, or in savor (fried and marinated in vinegar and onion). But there is also bass, bream, tuna, mussels, clams, cuttlefish and all manner of shellfish. Scallops are a favourite and are prepared delicately with local ingredients.

Eel is not to be forgotten, which is locally known as bisato. It is especially popular in and around Comacchio, where the Po meets the sea at the far south of the Veneto region.

Inland, baccalà (salt cod) and stoccafisso (dried cod, or stockfish) are used in many dishes, such as the ancient recipe from Vicenza in Veneto, Salt Cod in the Vicenza Style, and the robust dish from Trentino-Alto Adige, Stockfish in the Trentino Style.

MARINATED HERRING WITH ONIONS
ARINGHE MARINATE CON CIPOLLE

This is a typical fish dish of the Veneto region, which is left to marinate for at least 24 hours and is reminiscent of the kind of fish preparation carried out on board ships on long voyages. The dish is normally served cold, over hot polenta or with hot, buttered toast as an antipasto or snack. The flavour of the vinegar penetrates the whole dish, so it is essential to use one of a good quality for the best results.

1 In a large frying pan, bring the milk and water to the boil, then add the herrings. Cover and remove the pan from the heat. Allow the herrings to cook through in the residual heat for 5 minutes.

2 Remove the fish from the pan and place them on a rack over a bowl. Leave to drain and dry out for 30 minutes (alternatively, put them on a baking sheet in the oven heated to 200°C/400°F/Gas 6 to dry out for about 5 minutes).

3 Heat 45ml/3 tbsp oil in a pan, add the onions and fry until softened but not browned. Add the vinegar and boil for 2–3 minutes, then remove from the heat.

4 Fillet the herrings carefully, then arrange the fish fillets, onions and parsley in layers in a deep bowl.

5 When all the ingredients have been layered, cover with the remaining oil and leave to rest for at least 24 hours before serving.

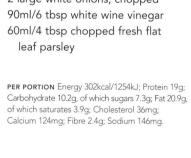

SERVES 4

600ml/1 pint/2½ cups full cream (whole) milk
600ml/1 pint/2½ cups water
4 whole herrings, gutted, scaled and washed
90ml/6 tbsp olive oil
2 large white onions, chopped
90ml/6 tbsp white wine vinegar
60ml/4 tbsp chopped fresh flat leaf parsley

PER PORTION Energy 302kcal/1254kJ; Protein 19g; Carbohydrate 10.2g, of which sugars 7.3g; Fat 20.9g, of which saturates 3.9g; Cholesterol 36mg; Calcium 124mg; Fibre 2.4g; Sodium 146mg.

SERVES 4

2 eggs
115g/4oz canned tuna in olive oil,
　drained and oil reserved
60ml/4 tbsp chopped fresh flat
　leaf parsley
½ garlic clove, finely chopped
juice of ½ lemon
75ml/5 tbsp fine dry breadcrumbs
30ml/2 tbsp olive oil
sea salt and ground black pepper

PER PORTION Energy 207kcal/867kJ; Protein 13.1g;
Carbohydrate 14.5g, of which sugars 0.5g; Fat 11.2g,
of which saturates 2g; Cholesterol 110mg;
Calcium 42mg; Fibre 0.4g; Sodium 261mg.

MOCK SPIDER CRAB IN THE TRIESTE STYLE
FALSA GRANCEOLA ALLA TRIESTINA

One of the greatest Venetian dishes is boiled freshly caught spider crab, locally known as granceola or grancevola, served in its shell and simply, but effectively, dressed with olive oil, lemon juice, seasoning and parsley. In Trieste, the capital of neighbouring Friuli-Venezia Giulia, the recipe given here is also traditionally served in the half-crab shell to give the impression that you are eating that great Venetian dish made with the rare spider crab. It can be served in shells, ramekins or other ovenproof dishes.

1 Add the eggs to a pan of boiling water and cook for 10 minutes. Drain, then put them into a bowl of cold water to cool. Peel and chop.

2 Flake the tuna and mix with the hard-boiled eggs, parsley and garlic. Stir in the lemon juice and enough of the reserved oil from the tuna to form a thick purée. Season with salt and pepper.

3 Preheat the grill (broiler) to medium. Arrange the tuna mixture in half-crab shells, or in other shells, small ramekins or ovenproof dishes, then cover with breadcrumbs and drizzle with the olive oil.

4 Slide under the grill and brown gently for 10–15 minutes.

PARCELS OF SOLE AND ROCKET
BOCCONCINI DI SOGLIOLA

This light and delicious recipe is from Friuli-Venezia Giulia, which is where speck comes from. Speck is a smoked ham that has been made in this region for centuries, using aromatic local wood in the smoking process. In this recipe, the smoky speck, the peppery rocket and the delicate fish combine to form a truly tasty dish. You could also use plaice fillets, or thin slices of monkfish tail. The speck is important, but if it is impossible to find, you can use prosciutto crudo instead.

1 Preheat the oven to 220°C/425°F/Gas 7. Lay the sole fillets out on a board. Line each one with a slice of speck, then season and sprinkle with the chopped rocket.

2 Roll up the fillets and secure with cook's string or wooden cocktail sticks (toothpicks).

3 Arrange the parcels in an oiled ovenproof dish, drizzle with the remaining oil and bake for 15 minutes, or until cooked through.

4 Remove the string or cocktail sticks and serve the parcels hot, accompanied by extra whole rocket leaves.

SERVES 4

4 soles, filleted (to make 16 fillets)
16 thin slices of speck or
    prosciutto crudo
1 bunch rocket (arugula) leaves,
    stalks removed, coarsely
    chopped, plus extra whole leaves,
    to serve
45ml/3 tbsp olive oil
sea salt and ground white pepper

PER PORTION Energy 174kcal/724kJ; Protein 18.9g; Carbohydrate 0.7g, of which sugars 0.6g; Fat 10.6g, of which saturates 1.5g; Cholesterol 52mg; Calcium 66mg; Fibre 0.5g; Sodium 410mg.

SERVES 4

45ml/3 tbsp plain (all-purpose) flour
800g/1¾lb pre-soaked salt cod
  (see Cook's Tip)
50g/2oz/¼ cup unsalted butter
30ml/2 tbsp sunflower oil
250g/9oz onions, thinly sliced
750ml/1¼ pints/3 cups full cream
  (whole) milk
4 salted anchovies, boned,
  washed and dried
30ml/2 tbsp chopped fresh flat
  leaf parsley
1 garlic clove, chopped
45ml/3 tbsp extra virgin olive oil
sea salt

COOK'S TIP

The fish will need to soak in fresh cold water for 4 days, changing the water 2–3 times each day. This will reconstitute the fish and remove the salt.

PER PORTION Energy 560kcal/2334kJ; Protein 44.5g; Carbohydrate 22.7g, of which sugars 12.7g; Fat 32.9g, of which saturates 13.3g; Cholesterol 147mg; Calcium 267mg; Fibre 1.2g; Sodium 319mg.

SALT COD IN THE VICENZA STYLE
BACCALÀ ALLA VICENTINA

From the lovely city of Vicenza comes this famous dish, considered by many to be the very best way to enjoy the real pleasures of baccalà or salt cod. In some versions of this ancient recipe, raisins or currants are added to the dish with the onions, or they are mixed into the oil with the anchovies, garlic and parsley towards the end of cooking. Like many other dishes of its kind, baccalà cooked this way always tastes better when reheated, and is traditionally served on top of white polenta.

1 Put the flour on a plate. Wash and trim the soaked fish, removing any skin or bones. Cut into chunks and toss lightly in the flour.

2 Heat the butter and sunflower oil in a large, heavy pan, add the onion slices and fry them gently until lightly browned.

3 Lay the floured fish in the pan and fry it gently on each side to brown it evenly.

4 Pour over the milk, then cover and simmer very gently for about 1½ hours.

5 Meanwhile, chop the anchovies finely and put into a bowl. Add the parsley, garlic and oil, and mix well. Season with salt if needed.

6 Stir the parsley and anchovy mixture into the pan. Cover and cook for a further 30 minutes, or until cooked through. Serve piping hot.

STOCKFISH IN THE TRENTINO STYLE
STOCCAFISSO ALLA TRENTINA

Similar to baccalà (salt cod), stoccafisso (stockfish) is dried cod, which was originally brought from much colder regions, such as the Scandinavian countries. The main difference between the two is that stoccafisso is dried by hanging it on special poles, then sometimes salted, whereas baccalà is cured by salting and is not previously air dried. Baccalà and stoccafisso are interchangeable for most recipes and it is generally a matter of personal preference which one is chosen to use in local dishes. The fish needs to be soaked overnight before use.

1 Drain and rinse the soaked stockfish. Bring a large pan of water to the boil, add the fish and cook it for 10 minutes over a medium heat.

2 Drain the fish, allow to cool then remove all the bones and skin completely. Cut the fish into small chunks and set it aside.

3 Heat the olive oil in a flameproof casserole, add the chopped onion and cook for 5–8 minutes, or until lightly browned.

4 Add the sliced celeriac to the casserole and turn it in the oil and onion until slightly browned, then add the potatoes. Stir everything together and season with salt and black pepper.

5 Add water to cover, cover the casserole with a lid and simmer gently over a low heat for about 15 minutes, or until half cooked. Meanwhile, preheat the oven to 180°C/350°F/Gas 4.

6 Remove the casserole from the heat and stir in the fish, garlic, bay leaves and cloves, then season with salt and black pepper.

7 Dot with the butter and pour over half the milk. Bake in the preheated oven for 15 minutes.

8 Remove from the oven and pour over the remaining milk. Return to the oven to bake for 20 minutes more, or until the milk has completely evaporated. Serve immediately.

SERVES 6

500g/1¼lb stockfish, soaked (see Cook's Tip)
30ml/2 tbsp olive oil
1 onion, chopped
1 small celeriac, thickly sliced
500g/1¼lb potatoes, peeled and thickly sliced
2 garlic cloves, finely chopped
2 bay leaves
4 cloves
25g/1oz/2 tbsp unsalted butter
600ml/1 pint/2½ cups full cream (whole) milk
sea salt and ground black pepper

COOK'S TIP

Soak the stockfish overnight in a bowl of half water and half milk, enough to cover the fish completely in the liquid.

PER PORTION Energy 300kcal/1256kJ; Protein 21.3g; Carbohydrate 27.7g, of which sugars 11.5g; Fat 12.3g, of which saturates 5.4g; Cholesterol 62mg; Calcium 159mg; Fibre 3.3g; Sodium 151mg.

SQUID COOKED IN ITS OWN INK
SEPPIE COL NERO

This dish never fails to create a sensation when it is served, because it is so dramatic in appearance, being mysteriously black in colour. In fact, the squid ink tastes much less strange than it looks – the flavour is not actually very strong. These days, it is increasingly hard to find squid with its ink sac intact within the body of the fish. If you can't find squid with its ink sac, you can buy the ink separately in small sachets, and this is perfectly fine to use for this recipe.

1 Wash the squid carefully, rinsing off any ink remaining on the body. Holding the body firmly, pull away the head and tentacles. If the ink sac is still intact, remove it carefully and set it aside.

2 Pull out and discard all the innards including the long transparent 'pen'. Peel off and discard the thin purple skin on the body, but keep the two small side fins. Slice across the head just under the eyes, reserving the tentacles. Discard the rest of the head.

3 Squeeze the tentacles at the head end to push out the round beak in the centre. Discard.

4 Rinse the pouch and tentacles well. Cut the squid into rings or strips.

5 Heat the olive oil in a frying pan over a medium heat and cook the garlic until softened. Add the squid pieces and cook to seal them on all sides.

6 Add the wine and simmer for 45 minutes. If the mixture appears dry, add a little water.

7 Add the ink from the sacs and cook for a further 45 minutes, or until tender. Season, sprinkle with the parsley and serve.

SERVES 4

800g/1¾lb very young, small
   whole squid
50ml/2fl oz/¼ cup extra virgin
   olive oil
2 garlic cloves, chopped
90ml/6 tbsp dry white wine
30ml/2 tbsp chopped fresh parsley
sea salt and ground black pepper

COOK'S TIPS

• If you prefer, ask your fishmonger to prepare the squid for you.
• If you buy the squid ink separately, you will need three sachets for this quantity of squid to achieve the correct degree of darkness, but you can use a little more, if you like. Add it to the stew as above.

PER PORTION Energy 254kcal/1065kJ; Protein 31.1g; Carbohydrate 2.7g, of which sugars 0.3g; Fat 11.8g, of which saturates 2g; Cholesterol 450mg; Calcium 43mg; Fibre 0.4g; Sodium 223mg.

SERVES 6

60ml/4 tbsp sunflower oil
1 large onion, chopped
2 garlic cloves, chopped
1 fresh rosemary sprig,
    leaves finely chopped
1kg/2¼lb squid, cleaned and sliced
225g/8oz can tomatoes, seeds
    removed, chopped
5ml/1 tsp tomato purée (paste)
pinch of ground cinnamon
pinch of freshly grated nutmeg
pinch of ground ginger
sea salt and ground black pepper
soft white polenta, to serve

COOK'S TIP

When using spices, it is worth remembering that they have a limited shelf life and soon lose their pungency. If possible, grind the spices just before use for the best results.

PER PORTION Energy 220kcal/924kJ; Protein 26.4g; Carbohydrate 5.9g, of which sugars 3.1g; Fat 10.3g, of which saturates 1.6g; Cholesterol 375mg; Calcium 33mg; Fibre 0.9g; Sodium 190mg.

SPICED SQUID CASSEROLE
SEPPIE IN UMIDO

A typical Venetian dish, this deliciously spicy squid casserole makes full use of the wide variety of traditional spices freely available in the region. It is truly representative of Venice's centuries-long history as a major spice-trading port. Traditionally, the casserole would be generously spooned over a helping of hot, soft white polenta, but it could also be served with a portion of equally sustaining rice or mashed potatoes, if you prefer.

1 Heat the oil in a large pan over a medium heat, add the onion and garlic, and fry for 5 minutes, until softened but not browned.

2 Add the rosemary, then the squid, and mix together. Pour over 500ml/17fl oz/2¼ cups water. Bring to the boil. Simmer for 45 minutes.

3 Add the tomatoes, tomato purée, salt, pepper and spices. Cover and simmer slowly for a further 45 minutes, or until the squid is tender and the sauce has thickened.

4 Serve the casserole hot over portions of soft white polenta, if you like.

WARM CUTTLEFISH SALAD WITH ROCKET
INSALATA TIEPIDA DI CALAMARI ALLA RUCOLA

Warm seafood salads are popular all along the Adriatic coast of Italy. This one, from Friuli-Venezia Giulia, is made especially tasty by the addition of anchovy paste and garlic, and has a finishing touch of rocket to add pepperiness to the dish. You could make the same salad using different types of seafood, such as octopus, squid, prawns (shrimp) or a mixture of fish and shellfish, including mussels and chunks of firm white fish. If the cuttlefish are small and tender, leave them whole rather than chopping them.

1 Bring a pan of salted water to the boil and add the peppercorns, half the parsley, the bay leaf and the wine.

2 Add the cuttlefish and cook at a gentle boil for 35–40 minutes, or until tender; the cooking time will depend on how large the fish are.

3 Meanwhile, chop the remaining parsley and mix with the anchovy paste and garlic. Mix in the lemon juice and oil, and season with salt.

4 Drain and chop the cuttlefish coarsely, then distribute between four plates. Pour over the oil and herb mixture, cover with a layer of rocket and serve immediately.

SERVES 4

5ml/1 tsp black peppercorns
handful of fresh flat leaf parsley
1 bay leaf
175ml/6fl oz/¾ cup dry white wine
600g/1lb 5oz cuttlefish, cleaned
    and cut into rings and tentacles
5ml/1 tsp anchovy paste
1 garlic clove, chopped
juice of ½ lemon
60ml/4 tbsp olive oil
1 bunch rocket (arugula), about
    3 handfuls
sea salt

PER PORTION Energy 243kcal/1011kJ; Protein 25.1g; Carbohydrate 0.7g, of which sugars 0.6g; Fat 12.4g, of which saturates 1.9g; Cholesterol 165mg; Calcium 137mg; Fibre 0.5g; Sodium 621mg.

60ml/4 tbsp plain (all-purpose) flour
1 medium-large fresh eel, skinned
1 onion, chopped
1 garlic clove, chopped
60ml/4 tbsp olive oil
30ml/2 tbsp white wine vinegar
1 bay leaf
sea salt
boiled potatoes, tossed in butter
  and chopped parsley, to serve

PER PORTION Energy 312kcal/1299kJ; Protein 15.1g; Carbohydrate 19.6g, of which sugars 5.8g; Fat 19.9g, of which saturates 3.8g; Cholesterol 113mg; Calcium 60mg; Fibre 1.9g; Sodium 70mg.

EEL COOKED IN THE VENETIAN STYLE
BISATO ALLA VENEZIANA

This is a very simple recipe for cooking eel, a fish that is plentiful in the ditches and lagoons of the Po Delta. The difficult part of the preparation of eel is the removal of its tough outer skin. You could ask your fishmonger to do this for you, or use a scouring pad to help you remove it. Traditionally, handfuls of coarse sand or rough ash dust would be used. Once complete, the process reveals a flesh that is deliciously tender and moist with a distinctive and quite delicate flavour.

1 Put the flour on a plate. Wash the eel, remove the guts, and cut the flesh into chunks. Coat lightly in the flour.

2 Put the onion, garlic and oil into a large, heavy pan, and fry gently until the onion is softened. Add the floured eel and brown the chunks all over.

3 Allow to cook for a further 2 minutes after browning, then add the vinegar, bay leaf and 2 tbsp water.

4 Cover and simmer gently for 20 minutes, or until the eel is completely softened, moistening it occasionally with a little water. Serve immediately, with boiled potatoes.

WRAPPED SCALLOPS
CAPESANTE IN CAMICIA

Scallops cooked this way taste absolutely wonderful, and are surprisingly simple to prepare. Their fresh sweetness is offset by the bitter flavour of the radicchio and the meatiness of the pancetta, and the finished dish looks very pretty too. It makes an excellent appetizer for eight people or a main course for four when served with some accompanying vegetables or salad. Serve the scallops with a chilled dry white wine such as the local Soave from around Verona in the Veneto region.

1 Wrap each scallop first in a slice of ham, then in a radicchio leaf, securing each one with a wooden cocktail stick (toothpick). Allow the pancetta to stick out slightly around the radicchio, if possible.

2 Brush each wrapped scallop lightly with a little extra virgin olive oil or melted pork fat.

3 Preheat the grill (broiler), or a hot griddle (the griddle will be hot when a little water splashed on to the surface evaporates instantly).

4 Cook for 5 minutes until the pancetta that is sticking out from the radicchio is crisp around the edges, turning twice or three times. Serve immediately, with lemon wedges.

SERVES 4

16 large scallops
16 paper-thin slices of pancetta
16 radicchio leaves
30ml/2 tbsp extra virgin olive oil
  or melted pork fat
lemon wedges, to serve

COOK'S TIP

You can use frozen scallops for this dish instead of fresh, if you prefer. Make sure you defrost them thoroughly before cooking.

PER PORTION Energy 299kcal/1247kJ; Protein 30.7g; Carbohydrate 3.8g, of which sugars 0.4g; Fat 17.9g, of which saturates 5g; Cholesterol 77mg; Calcium 39mg; Fibre 0.2g; Sodium 764mg.

SERVES 4

16 scallops with their shells, cleaned
 and prepared (see Cook's Tip)
175ml/6fl oz/¾ cup olive oil
3 garlic cloves, finely chopped
30ml/2 tbsp finely chopped fresh
 flat leaf parsley
25ml/1½ tbsp lemon juice
45ml/3 tbsp dry white wine
sea salt and ground black pepper
lemon wedges, to serve

COOK'S TIP

To prepare scallops in their
shells, scrub the shells in cold
water. Cut the hinge muscles
at the base using a knife. Lift
off the rounded shell. Scrape
away the beard-like fringe.
Remove the intestinal thread.
Ease the scallop from the
shell. Detach the orange coral
from the scallop and set aside.

PER PORTION Energy 367kcal/1526kJ; Protein 24.7g;
Carbohydrate 4.8g, of which sugars 1.2g; Fat 27g,
of which saturates 3.9g; Cholesterol 47mg;
Calcium 130mg; Fibre 2.5g; Sodium 197mg.

SCALLOPS COOKED IN THE VENETIAN STYLE
CAPESANTE ALLA VENETA

In this recipe, fresh scallops are gently poached in their own juices with white wine,
lemon juice and garlic to make the simplest of dishes. The sweet meatiness of the
shellfish is beautifully offset by the other flavours. Scallops are popular in Venice and
they feature in many rice and pasta dishes, or are served simply as in this recipe.
You can buy them cleaned and prepared from any good fishmonger – ask for the
shells for serving. You could also serve it as an appetizer for eight people.

1 Scrub the scallop shells and put them into
a low oven to warm. Heat the olive oil in a
frying pan, then add the chopped garlic and
the parsley. Fry together for 2–3 minutes.

2 Add the scallops (but not the corals) and
lower the heat to the very lowest setting.

3 Season, add the lemon juice and wine, then
simmer very gently for 8 minutes.

4 Add the corals and cook for 2 minutes more.
The scallops should be just firm and white.
Transfer the scallops back into their clean shells
and serve immediately, with lemon wedges.

POULTRY, MEAT AND GAME
POLLAME, CARNE E CACCIA

North-eastern Italy is the region that specializes in poultry, with countless delicious recipes, especially duck and goose. In the east, in Trentino-Alto Adige and Friuli-Venezia Giulia, pork, especially pork sausages that are very similar to those made in Austria and parts of Germany, and game, such as locally shot venison, are eaten more than almost anywhere else in the country and the style of cooking is very different too. Very little tomato is used in the warming casseroles and stews, and sauerkraut (or crauti, in Italian) is often served alongside meat dishes. Horsemeat is hugely popular all over the Veneto; many of the local butcher's shops are specialists in carne equina, and are clearly sign-posted as such. Other more unusual meats that are eaten in the Veneto include frog's legs and snails.

POULTRY, GOULASH AND RED WINE STEWS

Chicken, duck and other poultry are widely eaten in the Veneto and there are many methods of cooking them. Venetian Stuffed Duck, like Venetian Stuffed Chicken, is a centuries-old dish that uses a variety of classic Venetian ingredients for the stuffing. Duck, chicken and game tend to be served with a traditional sauce known as Salsa Peverada (see page 19). This sauce is a heady mix of strong flavours, including chicken livers, anchovies, bacon, lemon rind, garlic and white wine vinegar, which works with chicken and stands up surprisingly well to the richness of game and duck.

German- or Austrian-style sausages are a favourite in Friuli-Venezia Giulia and eastern Trentino-Alto Adige, reflecting the proximity and influence of neighbouring Austria.

Another dish that seems very far removed from the world-famous Italian menu is goulash, which is enjoyed in many forms in the north-east. Many other hearty beef stews are made in these regions, for example Venetian Beef Stew, which is rich and flavoursome, being cooked in a whole bottle of good-quality red wine. Other red wine stews use local game, such as the wonderful Guinea Fowl in Red Wine, which benefits from using a full-bodied wine from the region, such as Amarone. These rich, warming stews are often served with a good-sized portion of steaming polenta, which makes the meal extremely substanial and robust.

Pork is also eaten in these north-eastern regions. It is often prepared by being marinated in white wine, then cooked slowly in milk. Or it is made into rambasici, or Stuffed Savoy Cabbage Bundles, which is a classic dish in Friuli-Venezia Giulia.

FRIED VENETIAN CHICKEN
POLLO FRITTO ALLA VENETA

Although fried chicken exists as a traditional dish in many parts of Italy, in the Veneto the chicken is first marinated in a sour mix of lemon juice, parsley and salt to flavour it before coating it in egg and breadcrumbs for frying. The olive oil used in the northern regions tends not to be the intensely flavoured extra virgin that is used further south. Here, the much milder olive oil, from the second or third pressing, is used – and always more sparingly than in the south. Serve with a vegetable dish or salad.

1 Put the pieces of chicken into a large bowl and set aside. Pour the lemon juice into a small bowl, add the parsley and a pinch of salt, and mix together.

2 Pour this mixture all over the chicken, stir well, then leave to marinate for 50 minutes, turning the pieces frequently.

3 Put the beaten eggs into another large bowl and stir in a pinch of salt.

4 Remove the chicken from the marinade and immerse in the beaten egg. Leave to stand for 10 minutes.

5 Put the breadcrumbs on a plate. Take each piece of chicken out of the beaten egg and dip it into the breadcrumbs to coat it thoroughly all over.

6 Heat the oil in a deep pan to 180°C/350°F, until a cube of bread, dropped into the oil, turns golden in about 45 seconds. Add most of the sage, reserving a little to garnish, then fry the chicken pieces, in batches, first over a very high heat to seal, then over a lower heat until the chicken is cooked right through.

7 Serve hot, garnished with the reserved sage, with lemon wedges and a salad, if you like.

SERVES 4

1 chicken, about 1.6kg/3½lb, boned
   and cut into large chunks
juice of 2 large lemons
60ml/4 tbsp chopped fresh parsley
2 eggs, beaten
75ml/5 tbsp fine dried breadcrumbs
200ml/7fl oz/scant 1 cup olive oil
1 large sage sprig
sea salt
lemon wedges and a salad, to serve

VARIATION

Although not traditional, sunflower or vegetable oil could be used in place of the olive oil, and would be less expensive.

PER PORTION Energy 821kcal/3405kJ; Protein 45.6g; Carbohydrate 14.5g, of which sugars 0.5g; Fat 64.9g, of which saturates 13.5g; Cholesterol 310mg; Calcium 52mg; Fibre 0.4g; Sodium 324mg.

SERVES 4

1 oven-ready chicken, about
   1.6kg/3½lb
75g/3oz fatty pancetta or bacon,
   thinly sliced
7 fresh sage leaves
1 rosemary sprig
½ large onion, thickly sliced
30–45ml/2–3 tbsp olive oil
40g/1½oz/3 tbsp unsalted butter
250ml/8fl oz/1 cup warm
   chicken stock
sea salt

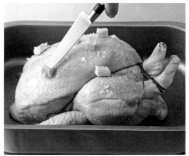

PER PORTION Energy 601kcal/2489kJ; Protein 43.3g;
Carbohydrate 0g, of which sugars 0g; Fat 47.4g,
of which saturates 15.8g; Cholesterol 250mg;
Calcium 16mg; Fibre 0g; Sodium 458mg.

VENETIAN STUFFED CHICKEN
POLASTRO IMBOTIO

In this recipe from the Veneto, a whole chicken is stuffed with a combination of bold tastes, including pancetta, rosemary, sage and onion, which permeate the flesh as it is cooked. Once it is juicy, tender and cooked all the way through, it is jointed and the stuffing ingredients are discarded. It is certainly worth splashing out on a good-quality free-range or organic chicken with lots of flavour for this simple but classic Venetian favourite.

1 Preheat the oven to 200°C/400°F/Gas 6. Wash and dry the chicken. Put the pancetta or bacon slices inside the cavity with the sage, rosemary and onion slices. Add a pinch of salt and sew the chicken closed with cook's string.

2 Lightly oil a roasting pan that the chicken will fit into snugly. Truss the chicken legs tightly together, crossing them over and tying them with cook's string, then lay it in the roasting pan. Lightly oil the chicken, then season with salt and dot with the butter.

3 Baste the chicken with 2–3 tbsp of chicken stock, then place it in the oven to roast for 1 hour, or until cooked through. Baste frequently throughout cooking.

4 Test the chicken is cooked by piercing the thickest part with the point of a knife; the juices should run clear and the flesh should be white, not pink. Remove the string and joint the chicken, discarding the filling ingredients. Serve the chicken with the pan juices poured over.

VENETIAN STUFFED DUCK
ANATRA COL PIEN

Sophisticated and elegant, this dish is one of the tastiest ways to serve duck. It is a very old recipe and one that makes the most of the wide variety of ingredients that have been available to the people of Venice for many centuries. The dish looks as good as it tastes as long as the duck has been boned properly. If you are not confident about this, ask your butcher to do it for you, or roast the duck whole and cook the stuffing separately. Serve with Salsa Peverada (see page 19), if you like.

1 To bone the duck, first cut out the wishbone and the wing tips. Lay the duck breast-side down with the back facing up, then, using a sharp knife, cut along the backbone. Pull the flesh away from the bone as you cut between the flesh and bone on one side of the bird. Don't cut into the skin.

2 Cut through the wing and thigh joints and between the breast meat and ribcage. Turn the bird around and repeat on the other side. Cut off the flesh from the breastbone. Cut the tendons at the end of the thigh and wing bones and scrape off the flesh along the bone. Remove the bone. Set the boned duck aside.

3 Preheat the oven to 180°C/350°F/Gas 4. Mix together the minced veal or chicken, the 115g/4oz chopped bacon or pancetta (reserving the extra rasher), the duck or chicken livers, 30ml/2 tbsp olive oil, parsley and breadcrumbs.

4 Put the Marsala into a small bowl, add the crumbled biscuits and stir until mushy. Pour this into the minced meat mixture.

5 Stir in the Parmesan cheese and candied mustard fruits, and season to taste with salt and pepper. Stir in the egg yolk.

6 Lay the prepared duck on a board, spoon this mixture into it and sew it closed with white cook's string.

7 In a small bowl, blend together the remaining olive oil, a little salt, the chopped rosemary and the chopped bacon rasher.

8 Put the stuffed duck into an oiled roasting pan and spread the rosemary mixture over it. Baste the duck with 2–3 tbsp wine and put it in the oven. Roast the duck for 1½ hours, basting it frequently with the wine (it may not be necessary to use all of the wine), until cooked. Test by piercing with a knife – the juices should run clear.

9 Transfer the duck to a warmed platter and carve. Serve with Salsa Peverada and cabbage, if you like.

SERVES 6

1 oven-ready duck, about 2kg/4½lb
115g/4oz veal escalope (US scallop) or chicken breast fillet, minced (ground)
115g/4oz, plus l rasher (strip), streaky (fatty) bacon or pancetta, finely chopped
1 duck liver or 2 chicken livers, trimmed and chopped
75ml/5 tbsp olive oil, plus extra for greasing
60ml/4 tbsp chopped fresh parsley
1 stale white bread roll, crusts removed, grated
75ml/5 tbsp Marsala
4 amaretti or 2 macaroons, crumbled
15ml/1 tbsp freshly grated Parmesan cheese
30–45ml/2–3 tbsp candied mustard fruits (mostarda di frutta), chopped
1 egg yolk
2 rosemary sprigs, leaves chopped
750ml/1¼ pint/3 cups dry white or red wine
sea salt and ground black pepper
Salsa Peverada (see page 19) and cabbage, to serve (optional)

PER PORTION Energy 569kcal/2361kJ; Protein 35.3g; Carbohydrate 1.6g, of which sugars 1.5g; Fat 45g, of which saturates 13.7g; Cholesterol 280mg; Calcium 52mg; Fibre 0g; Sodium 426mg.

GUINEA FOWL IN RED WINE
FARAONA AL VINO ROSSO

The Veneto is the one Italian region where poultry seems to be particularly celebrated as an ingredient, and many recipes exist for cooking duck, chicken, guinea fowl, goose and turkey. The most famous red wine of north-eastern Italy is Amarone, and it comes from the Veneto. A variety of Valpolicella, which is a blended wine of several grape varieties, Amarone is arguably one of Italy's three great red wines, the others being Barolo and Brunello di Montalcino. Naturally, the better the red wine used for cooking a dish such as this one, the better the finished results will be, and Amarone would be an obvious choice. Serve the guinea fowl on a bed of steaming hot polenta, for a warming winter supper.

SERVES 4

25g/1oz dried porcini mushrooms
1 large oven-ready guinea fowl, about 1kg/2¼lb
2 large onions, chopped
2 thick rashers (strips) pancetta or bacon, chopped
1 Italian sausage, chopped
25g/1oz plain (all-purpose) flour
500ml/17fl oz/2¼ cups full-bodied red wine, such as Amarone
50g/2oz/¼ cup unsalted butter
sea salt and ground black pepper
soft polenta, to serve
finely chopped fresh flat leaf parsley, to garnish

1 Put the porcini mushrooms into a bowl. Cover with hand-hot water, and leave to stand for 30 minutes, or until perfectly reconstituted and softened. Joint the guinea fowl into portions.

2 Cook the onions, pancetta and sausage together in a flameproof casserole over a medium heat until the onions are golden brown.

3 Add the jointed guinea fowl, sprinkle with the flour and mix together until hot, then add three-quarters of the red wine. Season with salt and pepper and boil for about 2 minutes to evaporate the alcohol.

4 Drain the mushrooms and add them to the casserole, then cover with a lid, lower the heat and simmer very gently for about 40 minutes, or until the guinea fowl is cooked through.

5 Remove the joints from the casserole and set them aside to keep warm. Remove the casserole from the heat. Push the cooked mixture from the casserole through a food mill.

6 Return the mixture to the casserole and heat over a medium heat. Stir well, adding the butter and remaining red wine, then allow to reduce to make a smooth sauce.

7 Serve the guinea fowl on top of steaming hot soft polenta, with the sauce poured all over it. Garnish with chopped fresh flat leaf parsley.

> **COOK'S TIP**
>
> You can reserve the soaking liquid from the porcini mushrooms to cook with in another recipe, if you like. Once softened, carefully remove the soaked porcini mushrooms from the bowl with a slotted spoon and allow the sediment in the bowl to resettle. Check over the mushrooms carefully for grit before using, then strain the liquid left in the bowl carefully through a very fine sieve (strainer) lined with kitchen paper or muslin (cheesecloth). Taste the liquid before using it to cook with, as it can sometimes be a little bitter.

PER PORTION Energy 586kcal/2449kJ; Protein 59.1g; Carbohydrate 13.1g, of which sugars 6.1g; Fat 24.2g, of which saturates 10.5g; Cholesterol 37mg; Calcium 115mg; Fibre 1.6g; Sodium 417mg.

SERVES 8

45ml/3 tbsp olive oil
500g/1¼lb lamb, trimmed of fat
    and cut into small cubes
200g/7oz pork, trimmed of fat
    and cut into small cubes
300g/11oz plain (all-purpose) flour,
    plus extra for dusting
50g/2oz/⅓ cup pork dripping
5 ripe tomatoes, peeled,
    seeded and finely chopped
    (see Cook's Tip)
1 garlic clove, finely chopped
45ml/3 tbsp chopped fresh flat
    leaf parsley
sea salt and ground black pepper

LAMB AND PORK PIE
PANADA D'AGNELLO E MAIALE

This traditional meaty pie from the countryside of the Veneto can also be made with many different kinds of meat that vary from kid, which is used in the springtime with artichokes, peas, ham and fresh herbs, to chunks of horsemeat for a much richer and more substantial dish. In all cases, the meat tends to remain quite chewy, so make sure it is cut into small cubes. The pie is good served cold, and is therefore a tasty and useful addition to a picnic spread.

1 Heat 30ml/2 tbsp of the oil in a wide frying pan, add the meat and fry until well browned all over. Put the meat into a sieve (strainer) to drain until required. Preheat the oven to 200°C/400°F/Gas 6.

2 Put the flour on to a work surface, make a hollow in the centre with your fist and put the dripping into the hollow.

3 Knead together gently with your fingers to make a smooth ball of dough, adding a little tepid water if necessary. Rest the dough, wrapped in clear film (plastic wrap), for 10 minutes in the refrigerator.

4 Roll out the dough on a floured surface as thinly as possible. Use two-thirds of it to line a 25cm/10in cake tin (pan) or oval pie dish. Re-roll out the remaining dough to make a lid.

5 Lay the browned meat in the tin or dish and cover with the tomatoes, garlic and parsley. Season, sprinkle with the remaining oil and cover with the prepared dough lid.

6 Moisten the edges of the pie and pinch to seal them carefully. Pierce the top in several places with a skewer to allow the steam to escape during cooking. Bake for 1½ hours, or until golden.

COOK'S TIP

To peel tomatoes, plunge them into boiling water for 30 seconds, then refresh in cold water. Peel away the skins – they should come away quite easily.

PER PORTION Energy 374kcal/1566kJ; Protein 21.6g; Carbohydrate 31.1g, of which sugars 2.5g; Fat 19g, of which saturates 7.7g; Cholesterol 69mg; Calcium 64mg; Fibre 1.8g; Sodium 78mg.

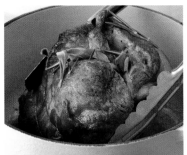

PORK COOKED IN MILK
MAIALE AL LATTE

First marinated in wine, pork is stewed slowly in milk and herbs in this recipe. It is a popular cooking method in the whole of the north of Italy; certain cuts of veal are also often cooked in this way. The meat ends up tasting deliciously sweet and is perfectly tender, and the cooked milk gives the sauce a very unusual texture. The milk will have curdled quite dramatically by the time the meat is ready, but rest assured that this is quite normal.

1 Put the meat in a non-metallic bowl, cover with the wine and leave to marinate in the refrigerator for between 6 hours and 2 days.

2 Remove the meat from the wine and pat dry with kitchen paper. Discard the wine.

3 Heat the butter in a large frying pan. Add the herbs and fry the meat until browned all over. Season with salt and pepper.

4 Transfer the meat to a large flameproof casserole and pour over the milk. Simmer over a low heat, covered, for 3 hours or until the meat is cooked through.

5 Remove the lid for the last 5 minutes to allow the liquid to reduce. Transfer the meat to a warmed platter, slice thickly and pour the sauce over the slices. Serve with braised radicchio and layered potatoes, if you like.

SERVES 4

1kg/2¼lb boned pork loin, shoulder
  or leg, tied with cook's string
550ml/18fl oz/2¼ cups dry white wine
50g/2oz/¼ cup butter
5 sage leaves
5 tiny rosemary sprigs
1 litre/1¾ pints/4 cups full cream
  (whole) milk
sea salt and ground black pepper

COOK'S TIP

Alternatively, cook this dish in the oven. Preheat the oven to 160°C/325°F/Gas 3. Place the casserole in the oven at step 4. Cook for 3 hours, removing the lid for the final 5 minutes.

PER PORTION Energy 679kcal/2834kJ; Protein 77.1g; Carbohydrate 3.3g, of which sugars 3.3g; Fat 29.2g, of which saturates 14g; Cholesterol 231mg; Calcium 103mg; Fibre 0g; Sodium 280mg.

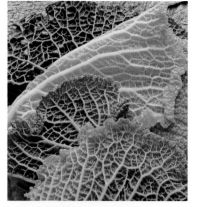

STUFFED SAVOY CABBAGE BUNDLES
RAMBASICI

This recipe from Friuli-Venezia Giulia has a dialect name that means 'escaped birds', as the swollen cabbage leaves are supposed to look like little birds hiding away from hunters' guns. You'll need only the green leaves from the cabbage, some of which will be large enough to cut in half, or even into quarters, once you have blanched them all. This makes a satisfying winter dish, and needs only a warm potato salad and some good red wine to make it into a delicious supper.

1 Select 12 of the unblemished outer leaves of the cabbage with care, blanch them for 1 minute in salted boiling water, then arrange them flat on a work surface, ready to fill. Set aside while you make the filling.

2 Mix together the minced meats, parsley, garlic, hard-boiled eggs, bread and salami in a small bowl. Divide the mixture among the cabbage leaves – there should be about 15ml/1 tbsp of filling in each.

3 Roll up each cabbage leaf around the filling, carefully seal closed with two cocktail sticks (toothpicks) and set aside.

4 Heat the vegetable oil or butter in a wide shallow pan and fry the sliced onion for 5–8 minutes over a medium-high heat, until well browned.

5 Remove the onion from the pan and set aside. Put the cabbage rolls, in a single layer, into the pan in which you cooked the onion. Cover with half the stock, bring to the boil, then reduce to a simmer and cook for 15 minutes.

6 Add the remaining stock to the pan and cook for a further 15 minutes.

7 Heat the olive oil in a separate pan and fry the breadcrumbs and Parmesan cheese until crisp.

8 Arrange all the rambasici on a warmed platter, sprinkle with the fried breadcrumb mixture and serve immediately.

SERVES 4

1 large Savoy cabbage
300g/11oz/scant 1½ cups lean minced (ground) pork
300g/11oz lean minced (ground) beef
50g/2oz parsley, leaves chopped
2 garlic cloves, finely chopped
2 hard-boiled eggs, peeled and finely chopped
2 slices brown bread, cut into very small cubes
3 slices salami, cut into small squares
90ml/6 tbsp vegetable oil or 50g/2oz/¼ cup unsalted butter
1 large onion, sliced
300ml/½ pint/1¼ cups meat stock
30ml/2 tbsp olive oil
30ml/2 tbsp dry breadcrumbs
30ml/2 tbsp freshly grated Parmesan cheese
sea salt and ground black pepper

> **VARIATION**
> ....
> You can omit the fried breadcrumbs, if you prefer, and lightly coat the finished cabbage rolls with a little tomato sauce instead.

PER PORTION Energy 756kcal/3143kJ; Protein 46.5g; Carbohydrate 30.9g, of which sugars 16.5g; Fat 50.3g, of which saturates 15.5g; Cholesterol 225mg; Calcium 290mg; Fibre 7g; Sodium 540mg.

BEEF WITH A SHALLOT VINAIGRETTE
MANZO CON VINAIGRETTE DI SCALOGNO

Although this is a modern recipe from Trentino-Alto Adige, it reflects the regional tradition of boiling meat. If you prefer, you could flash-fry or quickly grill the meat instead of immersing it in the boiling stock. The vinaigrette contains shallots and chives, which are both rare in southern Italian cuisine, and extra virgin olive oil (the area of Italy nearest to Trentino-Alto Adige that produces olive oil is around the shores of Lake Garda, in Lombardy).

1 To make the vinaigrette, mix the chopped shallots with the olive oil, chives, lemon juice and salt in a small bowl. Set aside.

2 Cut the beef fillet into eight equal slices. Bring the beef stock to a rolling boil in a shallow pan.

3 Immerse the beef slices in the boiling stock for 1 minute to just cook the outside.

4 Serve the hot beef slices on top of the salad leaves (a large handful for each serving), and divide the vinaigrette equally among the four portions. Serve immediately.

SERVES 4

400g/14oz beef fillet
250ml/8fl oz/1 cup beef stock
mixed salad leaves, to serve

FOR THE VINAIGRETTE
3 shallots, finely chopped
60ml/4 tbsp extra virgin olive oil
15ml/1 tbsp finely chopped chives
juice of 1 lemon
sea salt

PER PORTION Energy 279kcal/1159kJ; Protein 22.9g; Carbohydrate 1.2g, of which sugars 0.9g; Fat 20.3g, of which saturates 5.4g; Cholesterol 58mg; Calcium 9mg; Fibre 0.2g; Sodium 556mg.

SERVES 4

30–45ml/2–3 tbsp olive oil or
    30ml/2 tbsp pork fat
2 onions, finely chopped
5–12½ml/1–2½ tsp paprika
1kg/2¼lb stewing steak, cut into
    large cubes
about 600ml/1 pint/2½ cups meat
    stock (optional)
1 garlic clove, finely chopped
2.5ml/½ tsp dried marjoram
2.5ml/½ tsp ground cumin
115g/4oz pancetta, cubed
sea salt
polenta, to serve

PER PORTION Energy 638kcal/2654kJ; Protein 63.1g;
Carbohydrate 9.2g, of which sugars 5.6g; Fat 39g,
of which saturates 13.1g; Cholesterol 164mg;
Calcium 46mg; Fibre 1.4g; Sodium 527mg.

TYROLEAN GOULASH WITH POLENTA
GULASCH ALLA TIROLESE CON POLENTA

There are countless versions of this classic Austro-Hungarian stew all over the north-east of Italy. The main ingredients, despite all the variations on the basic recipe, are the meat and the paprika, which gives the dish its classic, deep brick-red colour. Naturally, paprika varies in intensity, so you may wish to add more or less depending on personal taste, but bear in mind that there needs to be enough for it to colour the finished dish, and that it is intended to be quite spicy. Serve over polenta.

1 Put the oil or pork fat in a large pan over a medium heat. Add the onions and cook for 5–8 minutes or until lightly browned.

2 Add the paprika and fry together for 1 minute. Add the meat and brown all over.

3 Add enough water or stock to just cover the meat, then cover and simmer gently for 2–3 hours, or until the meat is tender.

4 In a small bowl, mix together the garlic, marjoram and cumin.

5 In a small pan, fry the pancetta cubes until crisp.

6 When the meat is cooked through, stir the spice mixture and the crisp pancetta into the stew. Adjust the seasoning, if necessary, by adding a little salt to taste. Serve immediately.

VENETIAN BEEF STEW
PASTISSADA DE MANZO

This hearty dish originated on the peasant stoves of the Veneto. Although those dwelling in the coastal areas naturally preferred fish and shellfish as the major source of protein, inland meat would have occasionally graced the menus. A rich stew such as this one, on top of a mound of polenta, would have stretched a lot further and fed many more mouths. The idea of this quantity of meat feeding just four people would have seemed wildly extravagant only a century ago.

1 Put the whole piece of stewing beef in a large bowl. Add the onion, carrot, celery and red wine, then add the cloves, cinnamon and peppercorns.

2 Mix together, turning the meat in the marinade. Cover and chill for about 24 hours.

3 Remove the meat from the marinade, reserving the marinade. Blot away the excess liquid from the meat using kitchen paper.

4 Pierce the meat all over using the point of a sharp knife. Insert the chopped pancetta, lardons or bacon into the meat using your fingers.

5 Pour the marinade into a flameproof casserole and bring it to the boil over a high heat, then add the meat. Mix a ladleful of the marinade with the tomato purée and pour back into the casserole.

6 Cover with a lid and turn the heat down to the lowest setting, then simmer very gently for about 3 hours, or until the meat is falling apart. (Alternatively, transfer the casserole to the oven, preheated to 160°C/325°F/ Gas 3, for 3 hours.) Turn the meat in the marinade occasionally during the cooking process.

7 When the meat is cooked through and tender, remove it from the marinade and set it aside on a board or serving platter. Reserve the marinade remaining in the casserole.

8 Cook the contents of the casserole over a medium heat, uncovered, until it is reduced and slightly thickened. Adjust the seasoning, adding salt and pepper to taste.

9 Carve the meat and distribute it between individual plates, accompanied by a mound of soft polenta. Pour the sauce over the meat and serve hot.

SERVES 4 TO 6

1kg/2¼lb stewing beef, trimmed
1 large onion, thickly sliced
1 large carrot, sliced
1 large celery stick, cut into chunks
750ml/1¼ pints/3 cups red wine
3 cloves
a large pinch of ground cinnamon
2.5ml/½ tsp lightly crushed
    black peppercorns
115g/4oz thinly sliced pancetta,
    lardons or streaky (fatty) bacon,
    coarsely chopped
30ml/2 tbsp concentrated tomato
    purée (paste)
sea salt and ground black pepper
polenta, to serve

COOK'S TIPS

• For a rich and deep flavour, buy good-quality red wine.
• Remember to keep the meat barely simmering on a very low heat during the cooking process to ensure it remains extremely tender.

PER PORTION Energy 467kcal/1946kJ; Protein 42.2g; Carbohydrate 8.6g, of which sugars 6.9g; Fat 20.3g, of which saturates 7.9g; Cholesterol 109mg; Calcium 44mg; Fibre 1.8g; Sodium 377mg.

250g/9oz/2¼ cups yellow
    polenta flour
600ml/1 pint/2½ cups beef or
    chicken stock
75g/3oz pork fat, minced
    (ground) finely
2 Italian sausages, sliced into rounds
30ml/2 tbsp dried fine breadcrumbs
3 eggs, beaten
30–45ml/2–3 tbsp freshly grated
    Parmesan cheese
1 thick bacon rasher (strip) or
    pancetta slice, weight 50g/2oz
sea salt and ground black pepper
salad leaves, to serve

SAVOURY POLENTA CAKE
MACAFAM

This is a good example of a very plain recipe that would have been eaten by the poorer population of the Veneto countryside rather than by the nobility of the grand households of Venice. It uses the basic starch maize meal, but instead of boiling it in water to make polenta, the flour is mixed with stock to make a smooth paste before it is combined with other ingredients and baked into a savoury cake. Note the use of the bacon for greasing the cake tin, which reflects the fact that no butter or oil would have been available. You can, of course, use oil for greasing if you prefer.

1 Preheat the oven to 180°C/350°F/Gas 4. Pour the polenta flour into a bowl and add the cold stock, stirring gently and constantly to achieve a smooth paste.

2 Stir in the minced pork fat, the sliced sausages, breadcrumbs, beaten eggs and Parmesan cheese. Season with salt and pepper.

3 Use the bacon or pancetta to grease a 25cm/10in cake tin (pan).

4 Pour in the polenta mixture and bake in the preheated oven for about 35 minutes, or until cooked through and golden brown.

5 Serve piping hot, with salad leaves.

PER PORTION Energy 599kcal/2494kJ; Protein 16.1g; Carbohydrate 61.4g, of which sugars 0.7g; Fat 32.1g, of which saturates 11.4g; Cholesterol 174mg; Calcium 54mg; Fibre 1.9g; Sodium 448mg.

LIVER COOKED IN THE VENETIAN STYLE
FEGATO ALLA VENEZIANA

Calf's liver cooked this way is a real classic of Venetian meat cuisine. The quantity of onions used for the dish might seem enormous when raw, but they are cooked very slowly to become almost a sticky jam, which will be topped by the sautéed liver. It really is imperative that the calf's liver is as fresh as possible; it should be shiny and have no strong smell when raw. Serve with mounds of fluffy mashed potato or soft white polenta.

1 Trim the liver with care, pulling off the transparent, rind-like skin from around each slice. Rinse the onions in cold running water, then drain and pat dry.

2 Heat the oil and butter in a heavy frying pan over a very low heat and gently fry the onions and parsley, covered, for 1 hour, until shiny and soft. Stir frequently to avoid sticking or burning.

3 Increase the heat and add the liver to the onions. Brown the liver slices quickly on both sides and pour the wine over as it browns. The liver will cook in about 5 minutes. Season well with salt and pepper.

4 Place a mound of mashed potato on each plate, and top it with the cooked onions and then the liver. Serve, sprinkled with parsley.

SERVES 4

500g/1¼lb calf's or lamb's liver, cut into very thin slices
750g/1lb 10oz red onions, very finely sliced
75ml/2½fl oz/⅓ cup vegetable oil
25g/1oz/2 tbsp unsalted butter
60ml/4 tbsp chopped fresh parsley, plus extra to garnish
175ml/6fl oz/¾ cup dry white wine
sea salt and ground black pepper
mashed potato, to serve

PER PORTION Energy 465kcal/1932kJ; Protein 27.5g; Carbohydrate 17.1g, of which sugars 10.8g; Fat 24.2g, of which saturates 8.2g; Cholesterol 552mg; Calcium 61mg; Fibre 2.6g; Sodium 149mg.

VEGETABLES, EGGS AND CHEESE
VERDURE, UOVA E FORMAGGIO

It may seem unusual that the tomato is almost completely absent in the cooking of north-eastern Italy, considering it is an ingredient that is used widely in the other regions and almost synonymous with Italy when thinking of the world-famous classics. In Trentino-Alto Adige, where the cuisine leans heavily on its Austro-Hungarian influences, cabbage is popular, and in all three regions potatoes and beans are used extensively. Radicchio is perhaps the most typical vegetable of Friuli-Venezia Giulia and Veneto, where it is used in soups, risottos and pasta sauces, or is served as an accompaniment or added to salads. Pumpkin is also very popular, and brightens up many dishes with its brilliant colour. Vegetables are combined with eggs to make nutritious frittatas, and local Alpine cheeses are a speciality, although the wonderful Parmesan is still used in many dishes.

ASPARAGUS, RADICCHIO AND POTATO FRITTERS

Eggs are a staple food in the north-east of Italy, just as they are across many other regions. They are inexpensive and nutritious, and can be combined with regional cheeses or seasonal vegetables to make flavoursome and sustaining frittatas, or flat omelettes. In this area, the local favourite dish, risotto, is specially prepared in order to be added to the egg mixture, making it hearty enough to be served as a meal on its own. Frittatas could also be accompanied by a side salad or some crusty bread to make them into a nourishing main course dish.

The vegetables that are eaten in this corner of Italy tend to be hardy root vegetables and nourishing greens, far removed from the delicate sun-ripened tomatoes, aubergines and courgettes (zucchini) that grow so well in the south. Cabbage, artichokes, asparagus, potatoes and onions are common in the culinary repertoire of the north-east, as well as the revered radicchio. The most common varieties are radicchio di Chioggia; radicchio di Verona; and radicchio di Treviso, which is the most highly prized type. This wonderful, bitter-tasting, red-leaved vegetable is used in a multitude of recipes, from soups and antipasti dishes to pasta sauces and risottos, as well as on its own as an accompanying vegetable.

The range of Alpine cheeses produced in Trentino-Alto Adige is vast, numbering over 60 different types of cheese that are made with cow's, ewe's or goat's milk, or combinations of these. The most important cheeses of the area are Asiago, a strong nutty cheese from the Veneto, and Montasio from Friuli, which has been prepared in the same simple way in the area since the 13th century.

RICE AND ASPARAGUS FRITTATA
FRITTATA DI RISO AGLI ASPARAGI

The classic flat omelette, so popular in its various forms all over Italy, is an ideal way to make a few ingredients go a little further, and is also useful for using up leftovers. This is a fairly sophisticated version of the dish, insofar as the risotto is made especially for the frittata, with delicious results. A similar version could also be made with leftover risotto that is simply mixed into beaten eggs. Serve with a salad and a light red wine, or make it a more substantial dish with some crusty bread.

1 Heat 65g/2½oz/5 tbsp butter in a large pan, add the asparagus, onion and speck, and fry together gently over a low-medium heat for 5–8 minutes, or until the onion is softened.

2 Add the risotto rice to the pan and mix together for about 5 minutes, or until the rice grains are crackling and well toasted.

3 Bring the stock to the boil in a separate pan and keep it at simmering point.

4 Add the stock to the rice, a ladleful at a time, and cook, stirring constantly, allowing each ladleful to be absorbed before adding the next.

5 After about 20 minutes the rice should be tender and cooked through. Remove the pan from the heat, season to taste and transfer to a bowl. Allow to cool, stirring frequently.

6 Whisk the eggs in a large bowl, then whisk in the Parmesan cheese. Add the cooked rice and mix thoroughly together.

7 Melt the remaining butter in a large non-stick frying pan and pour in the mixture. Shake the pan to flatten and even out the mixture, pulling the liquid egg into the centre as you work. Cook until the underside is browned and firm.

8 Turn over the frittata by covering the pan with a large lid or plate and then turning the pan over. Lift off the pan and put it back on the heat, then carefully slide the frittata (with the uncooked side underneath) back into the hot pan using both hands to steady the process.

9 Continue to cook the frittata until golden brown and firm on the underside. This will take less time than the first side.

10 Slide the frittata out on to a clean platter and serve hot, accompanied by salad leaves, if you like.

SERVES 4

75g/3oz/6 tbsp butter
300g/11oz asparagus tips,
    roughly chopped
1 small onion, finely chopped
115g/4oz speck, chopped
115g/4oz/generous ½ cup
    risotto rice
about 600ml/1 pint/2½ cups
    vegetable stock
6 eggs
50g/2oz/⅔ cup freshly grated
    Parmesan cheese
sea salt and ground black pepper
salad leaves, to serve (optional)

VARIATION

If you cannot get hold of speck, you could use Parma ham instead.

PER PORTION Energy 463kcal/1924kJ; Protein 24.2g; Carbohydrate 25.9g, of which sugars 2.6g; Fat 29.3g, of which saturates 15.4g; Cholesterol 358mg; Calcium 227mg; Fibre 1.5g; Sodium 728mg

RADICCHIO FRITTATA
FRITTATA DI RADICCHIO

The cream in this frittata softens the bitter taste of the radicchio leaves and enhances the texture of the finished dish by giving it density, and Parmesan cheese adds richness. The frittata is made in the traditional way: cooking the flat omelette on one side, then flipping it over and slipping it back into the hot pan to cook on the other side. It's lovely served as a flavoursome lunch with some thinly sliced fried potatoes, a side salad or some extra radicchio.

1 Whisk the cream with the Parmesan cheese and eggs, then season with salt.

2 Heat the oil and butter in a wide, non-stick pan. Mix the radicchio into the egg mixture, then pour it into the hot pan.

3 Shake the pan to flatten and even out the mixture, pulling the liquid egg into the centre as it cooks, and rocking the pan from side to side. Cook until the underside is browned and firm.

4 Turn over the frittata by covering the pan with a large lid or plate and then overturning the pan. Lift off the pan and put back on the heat, then carefully slide the frittata (uncooked side underneath) back into the hot pan using both hands to steady the process.

5 Continue to cook the frittata until golden brown and firm on the underside. This will take less time than the first side. Slide out on to a clean platter and serve hot, with some fried potatoes and extra radicchio, if you like.

SERVES 4

90ml/6 tbsp single (light) cream
250g/9oz/3 cups freshly grated
   Parmesan cheese
5 eggs, beaten
45ml/3 tbsp olive oil
25g/1oz/2 tbsp unsalted butter
5 heads of radicchio di Treviso, sliced
   into strips, plus extra to serve
sea salt and ground black pepper
thinly sliced fried potatoes, to serve

> **COOK'S TIP**
> ....
> • Use a non-stick pan for this recipe, as the cheese can cause the frittata to stick during cooking, which makes it difficult to keep it intact.
> • Make sure you have a flat lid or plate larger than the pan ready before you begin.

PER PORTION Energy 539kcal/2236kJ; Protein 33.1g; Carbohydrate 0.9g, of which sugars 0.9g; Fat 45g, of which saturates 22g; Cholesterol 327mg; Calcium 807mg; Fibre 0g; Sodium 827mg.

150g/5oz pork belly
500g/1¼lb fresh borlotti
  beans, podded
300g/11oz radicchio leaves,
  coarsely chopped
a drizzle of olive oil, to taste
sea salt and ground black pepper
4 slices of grilled (broiled) yellow
  polenta, to serve (optional)

COOK'S TIP

You can use dried borlotti beans instead of fresh, if you like. You will need 250g/9oz/1⅓ cups. Leave the beans to soak overnight, then rinse and boil them in fresh water for about 5 minutes. Drain, then rinse and use as above.

PER PORTION Energy 493kcal/2079kJ; Protein 34g; Carbohydrate 56.4g, of which sugars 4.4g; Fat 16.2g, of which saturates 5.4g; Cholesterol 27mg; Calcium 149mg; Fibre 20.3g; Sodium 52mg.

RADICCHIO WITH BEANS
RADICCHIO E FAGIOLI

This bitter, red-leafed vegetable is enormously popular all over the Veneto. Of the three most common varieties, radicchio di Chioggia is in the form of a tight ball; radicchio di Verona is floppy and lettuce-like; and radicchio di Treviso, perhaps the best-loved, has long, narrow leaves. Any of these can be used in this simple peasant recipe – a classic example of a dish where the protein is provided by a modest amount of meat, supplemented by beans. This makes it both cheaper and more healthy, while still being full of rich flavours. The radicchio needs barely any cooking and is simply allowed to wilt in the heat of the stew. It can be served on top of grilled or fried polenta, or alongside a meat dish, such as a roast or casserole.

1 Put the pork belly into a large pan with the beans and sufficient water to cover generously. Bring to the boil and cook gently, uncovered, for about 40 minutes, or until the beans are soft. (There should be very little liquid left in the pan and it should not be necessary to drain it. If it seems watery, boil it for a little longer to reduce the liquid.) Add a pinch of salt.

2 Remove the pork belly from the pan, chop it coarsely and set it aside.

3 Mix the radicchio into the beans, crushing the beans with a fork. Return the chopped pork belly to the pan, and stir well.

4 Add olive oil and season to taste. Serve hot or cold, on a slice of yellow polenta, if you like.

VENETIAN-STYLE TREVISO RADICCHIO
RADICCHIO DI TREVISO ALLA VENETA

This dish is usually served alongside grilled meats. It is particularly good with a grilled horsemeat steak, which is very popular locally, as the bitterness of the leaves and the sour tang of the vinegar act as a good foil for the sweet flavour of the meat. It is also good with grilled or fried calf's liver or with grilled cheese, for a lighter meal. This variety of radicchio is highly prized all over Italy and is used in a great many dishes, but another type of radicchio can be substituted if necessary.

1 Heat the oil in a frying pan, add the onion and pancetta, and fry until the pancetta is brown and crispy.

2 Add the radicchio leaves, mix together and season with salt and pepper.

3 Add the vinegar, then cook gently, stirring frequently, for about 15 minutes, or until the radicchio is soft and wilted.

4 Serve hot, with some soft yellow polenta, or as an accompaniment to a meat dish.

SERVES 4

60ml/4 tbsp olive oil
1 small onion, chopped
75g/3oz smoked pancetta,
   cut into thick, short strips
675g/1½lb radicchio di Treviso,
   leaves separated
30ml/2 tbsp red wine vinegar
sea salt and ground black pepper
yellow polenta, to serve (optional)

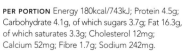
PER PORTION Energy 180kcal/743kJ; Protein 4.5g; Carbohydrate 4.1g, of which sugars 3.7g; Fat 16.3g, of which saturates 3.3g; Cholesterol 12mg; Calcium 52mg; Fibre 1.7g; Sodium 242mg.

SERVES 12

2kg/4½lb button (pearl) onions,
  washed and unpeeled
250ml/8fl oz/1 cup olive oil
200g/7oz/1 cup sugar
500g/1¼lb canned tomatoes,
  seeded and chopped
50g/2oz dark (bittersweet) cooking
  chocolate (minimum 70 per cent
  cocoa solids), grated coarsely
2 bay leaves
4 cloves
350ml/12fl oz/1½ cups dry white wine
sea salt and ground black pepper

COOK'S TIP

To preserve the onions, remove
them from the roasting pan
with a slotted spoon and
transfer to hot, sterilized jars.
Put the roasting pan on the hob
and heat to reduce the liquid,
then pour in the jars to fill to
the rim. Screw the lids on to the
jars, then boil them in a pan of
water for 15 minutes to further
sterilize them. Store in the
refrigerator. Use within 1 month.

PER PORTION Energy 268kcal/1117kJ; Protein 2.6g;
Carbohydrate 35g, of which sugars 30.6g; Fat 13g,
of which saturates 2.4g; Cholesterol 0.6mg;
Calcium 56mg; Fibre 2.7g; Sodium 10.6mg.

VENETIAN-STYLE STEWED BUTTON ONIONS
CIPOLLINE ALLA VENETA

These onions are served as an antipasto or as an accompanying vegetable with a
simple meat dish such as a lightly fried calf's liver. They are traditionally made in
great quantities and then preserved in jars and used as a chutney or accompaniment
to cheese or cured meats. The flavours of the ingredients in this recipe blend
together really well. Button onions are found at all good greengrocers and market
stalls in Italy, but pickling onions about the size of a walnut make a good substitute.

1 Bring a large pan of salted water to a rolling
boil, add the onions and boil them hard for
5–10 minutes, or until tender.

2 Drain, cool and peel carefully, leaving them
whole. Preheat the oven to 180°C/350°F/Gas 4.

3 Pour the oil into a roasting pan large
enough to take all the onions, and set over
medium heat. Heat gently for 5 minutes, then
gently stir in the sugar and allow it to brown,
stirring constantly over a low heat.

4 Dry the onions in a clean dish towel and add
them to the oil and sugar. Mix carefully
together to coat the onions completely, then
add the tomatoes, chocolate, bay leaves,
cloves and wine. Stir and simmer for about
5 minutes, then transfer to the oven and bake
for a further 5 minutes.

5 Take the roasting pan out of the oven, stir
and season. The onions can be served hot or
cold, or preserved in clean, sterilized jars for
later use (see Cook's Tip).

ASPARAGUS IN THE VENETIAN STYLE
ASPARAGI ALLA VENETA

The area of Bassano del Grappa, in the Veneto, is famous for producing phenomenally good asparagus. This recipe makes a dish that is good for serving alongside cold poached fish or with meats such as thinly sliced roasted ham or rare roast beef. Try to pick asparagus spears that are not too thick, as they tend to have less flavour than those that have a firm stem of medium thickness. The olive oil needs to have a gentle flavour without too much bite or pepperiness.

1 Add the eggs to a pan of boiling water and cook for 10 minutes. Drain the eggs and put them into a bowl of cold water to cool.

2 Snap off any woody ends from the asparagus stalks at the point where they break easily. Tie into four bundles and boil them upright in a tall pan with plenty of salted water for 8 minutes.

3 Meanwhile, peel the hard-boiled eggs and mash them in a small bowl. Add the vinegar, oil, salt and pepper, and mix together thoroughly.

4 Arrange the cooked asparagus in a serving dish, spoon over the dressing and serve immediately, while still hot.

SERVES 4

3 eggs
700g/1lb 9oz asparagus
5ml/1 tsp white wine vinegar
60ml/4 tbsp olive oil
sea salt and ground black pepper

PER PORTION Energy 253kcal/1046kJ; Protein 14.5g; Carbohydrate 3.5g, of which sugars 3.3g; Fat 20.4g, of which saturates 4.1g; Cholesterol 285mg; Calcium 90mg; Fibre 3g; Sodium 107mg.

SERVES 4

12 globe artichokes
juice of 1 lemon
100ml/3½fl oz/scant ½ cup olive oil
60ml/4 tbsp finely chopped fresh
   flat leaf parsley
1 garlic clove, finely chopped
200ml/7fl oz/scant 1 cup chicken
   or vegetable stock
sea salt and ground black pepper

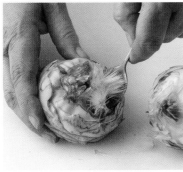

PER PORTION Energy 131kcal/542kJ; Protein 0.6g;
Carbohydrate 0.8g, of which sugars 0.8g; Fat 14g,
of which saturates 1.9g; Cholesterol 0mg;
Calcium 46mg; Fibre 1.2g; Sodium 34mg.

VENETIAN-STYLE BRAISED ARTICHOKE HEARTS
FONDI DI CARCIOFI ALLA VENETA

The market at the Rialto in Venice has mountains of artichokes for sale when the season is right, and the market traders will happily prepare them for you, saving you the trouble and time. Frozen artichoke hearts are widely available and save a lot of work, but they simply don't have the same intense flavour of the fresh vegetable. Although learning to prepare them for cooking might be hard work the first few times you try, it soon becomes easy.

1 Prepare the artichokes by removing all the outer leaves and trimming right down to the heart. Scrape out the choke from the centre and leave just 1cm/½in of leaf stump around the edge.

2 Put the prepared artichokes in a bowl of water with the lemon juice.

3 Heat the oil in a large pan, add the parsley and garlic, and fry together, stirring frequently, for 5 minutes.

4 Add the artichokes, basting them with the oil, then pour over the stock. Season, cover tightly and simmer for 30 minutes, or until tender. Serve hot, with the pan juices.

VICENZA-STYLE STEWED CABBAGE
CAVOLO ALLA VICENTINA

This simple dish of stewed cabbage is a tasty accompaniment for any pork dish, including grilled Italian sausages. The variety of apple usually chosen for this recipe is similar to a russet but is known in Italy as a renetta. It is squat and rosy with a rough, brown crown around the stalk. The type of cabbage traditionally used is called cappuccio in Italy, and is not as coarse-leafed as a Savoy, although Savoy cabbage can also be used in the recipe.

1 Heat the oil and butter together in a large pan over medium heat and add the onion, garlic and pancetta. Fry for 5–8 minutes, or until the onion is softened and the pancetta is lightly browned.

2 Add the cabbage and apple, and mix everything together thoroughly. Season, cover tightly and simmer gently for 45 minutes, or until the cabbage is tender, stirring occasionally. Serve hot.

SERVES 4

60ml/4 tbsp olive oil
25g/1oz/2 tbsp unsalted butter
1 large onion, chopped
1 garlic clove, chopped
115g/4oz pancetta, cubed
1.5kg/3¼lb green cabbage, cored and roughly chopped
1 eating apple, peeled, cored and sliced
sea salt and ground black pepper

PER PORTION Energy 333kcal/1378kJ; Protein 10g; Carbohydrate 20.5g, of which sugars 19.9g; Fat 23.7g, of which saturates 7.3g; Cholesterol 33mg; Calcium 189mg; Fibre 8.2g; Sodium 436mg.

400g/14oz aubergines (eggplants),
    cut into chunks
75g/3oz/6 tbsp unsalted butter
75ml/5 tbsp extra virgin olive oil
1 garlic clove, peeled and left whole
300g/11oz small onions, sliced
500g/1¼lb yellow and red (bell)
    peppers, cut into chunks
300g/11oz small tomatoes, chopped
90ml/6 tbsp dry white wine
sea salt
chopped fresh flat leaf parsley,
    to garnish

VARIATION

If you prefer, you can leave out
the aubergines and onions, and
use only peppers and garlic.

PER PORTION Energy 248kcal/1025kJ; Protein 2.5g;
Carbohydrate 12.4g, of which sugars 10.9g; Fat 20.2g,
of which saturates 8.2g; Cholesterol 29mg;
Calcium 33mg; Fibre 3.9g; Sodium 105mg.

STEWED VENETIAN PEPPERS
PEPERONATA ALLA VENEZIANA

This is the Venetian version of a dish that is made all over the country, especially at
the start of the autumn, when the markets are filled with enormously juicy, brightly
coloured peppers of every shape and size. The texture of the finished dish is soft
and squashy, almost like jam. It is important to buy sweet peppers and to keep
everything moist during the cooking process. This dish is fabulous as an
accompaniment to chicken or fish, or served on its own as part of an antipasto.

1 Put the aubergine chunks into a colander
and sprinkle with salt. Put a small plate on top
and weight it down with a can. Leave it for
30 minutes. Rinse and drain.

2 Heat the butter and oil in a large pan, add
the garlic and fry until browned. Discard the
garlic and add the onions.

3 Cook the onions until just soft, then add the
aubergines, the peppers and the tomatoes.
Sprinkle with the wine and add salt to taste.

4 Cover and simmer gently over a low heat for
1 hour, stirring frequently. Serve the peppers
hot or cold, garnished with chopped fresh flat
leaf parsley.

POTATO AND CHEESE GRATIN
GRATIN POLESANO

This recipe is for a complete supper dish, although it can also be served as a side dish for roast chicken or something similarly plain. Fontina cheese comes from Piedmont and is deliciously nutty and melts perfectly when cooked. Good substitutes could be Emmenthal or Gruyère, or even the main cheese of this region, Asiago. Extra stock might be needed to cook the potatoes without them drying out, depending on the type of potatoes used and the thickness of the dish.

1 Butter the sides and base of a deep, flameproof and ovenproof dish using 10g/¼oz/½ tbsp butter. Pour half the stock into the buttered dish and bring to the boil.

2 Remove from the heat and arrange half the potatoes in the dish, making sure they are covered by the stock. Return to the heat and cook gently for 10–15 minutes, until the stock has evaporated and potatoes are tender . Preheat the oven to 180°C/350°F/Gas 4.

3 Cover the potatoes with half the Fontina cheese and half the pancetta, season and cover with the remaining sliced potatoes. Pour over the remaining stock.

4 Finish with the remaining Fontina cheese and pancetta, dot the top with the rest of the butter and sprinkle with salt and pepper.

5 Bake for 20 minutes, or until the potatoes are tender and the top is golden.

SERVES 4 TO 6

25g/1oz/2 tbsp unsalted butter
475ml/16fl oz/2 cups chicken
   or beef stock
1kg/2¼lb potatoes, peeled
   and very thinly sliced
300g/11oz Fontina cheese, sliced
150g/5oz pancetta, thinly sliced
sea salt and ground black pepper

PER PORTION Energy 424kcal/1771kJ; Protein 19.5g; Carbohydrate 26.9g, of which sugars 2.2g; Fat 26.2g, of which saturates 15.3g; Cholesterol 74mg; Calcium 382mg; Fibre 1.7g; Sodium 726mg.

SERVES 4

8 large potatoes, peeled
  (see Cook's Tip)
25g/1oz/¼ cup plain
  (all-purpose) flour
90ml/6 tbsp full cream (whole) milk
60ml/4 tbsp freshly grated
  Parmesan cheese
200ml/7fl oz/scant 1 cup olive oil
sea salt

COOK'S TIP

It is preferable to use potatoes that are a few days old for this recipe, rather than fresh ones, as they will withstand the grating process better.

PER PORTION Energy 651kcal/2715kJ; Protein 12.3g; Carbohydrate 54.2g, of which sugars 5.1g; Fat 44.2g, of which saturates 9.2g; Cholesterol 18mg; Calcium 233mg; Fibre 3.2g; Sodium 209mg.

TRENTINO POTATO FRITTERS
TORTEI DI PATATE

This Trentino version of potato rösti is usually served piping hot with a platter of local cheeses and plenty of the local red wine, called Marzemino. Crisp on the outside and deliciously soft on the inside, the fritters are well flavoured with Parmesan cheese and incredibly moreish. They are equally tasty if you make them with different kinds of cheese, such as the sweet nutty types: Fontina, Emmenthal or Gruyère. You can also use sunflower oil instead of the traditional olive oil for frying.

1 Grate the potatoes coarsely, then mix them with the flour, milk, Parmesan cheese and salt.

2 Heat the olive oil in a large frying pan. Shallow-fry spoonfuls of the potato mixture to make fritters.

3 Turn the fritters over once they are golden and crisp on the underside and finish cooking on the other side.

4 Drain thoroughly on kitchen paper and sprinkle with a little salt before serving.

DESSERTS AND BAKING
DOLCI

When thinking about the dessert course in the north-east of Italy, the specialities that immediately spring to mind are the many sweet fritters that form an important part of the famous Venetian Carnevale. These can be simple, homely cakes; light, flaky strudels filled with apples and raisins; or traditional biscuits made from age-old recipes, using the vast range of spices that Venetians love. These are certainly not the regions for refreshing ice cream or frozen desserts. Here you are more likely to indulge yourself with rich, eggy, buttery cakes and pastries, which are sometimes filled with pears or apples, and often delicately laced with cinnamon, cloves and nutmeg. This was one of the first areas of Italy to use sugar instead of honey in desserts, and some recipes also use molasses and treacle.

SPICE-FILLED COOKIES AND CARNIVAL FRITTERS

The Austrian and German tradition of baking hearty cakes and delicate pastries really comes into its own in both Friuli and Trentino-Alto Adige. These sit alongside the somewhat solid Venetian specialities like deep-fried custard (crema fritta) as well as many other sweet fritters. Pandoro, from the beautiful city of Verona, symbolizes Christmas like few other cakes can. A craggy mountain topped with snow-white sugar, it even looks festive. It's extremely difficult to make, so Italians tend to buy good, commercially produced Pandoro from their local baker or supermarket, rather than baking it themselves.

Other local specialities include Gubana, which is a traditional pastry from Friuli-Venezia Giulia that somewhat resembles a strudel, although not as light and flaky, and generally comes with a minced apple filling and plenty of grappa. There are, however, other variations on this basic theme, including one that features pumpkin.

Trieste, with its mid-European feel, more Austrian than Italian, has always been famous for its café society and was one of the first places in Italy to really take to coffee. The Trieste tourist board recommends three historic cafés: Caffè Tommaseo, Caffè San Marco and Caffè Pasticceria Pirona. Excellent coffee and chocolate are served in these cafés, and the latter has been awarded a prize for the best hot chocolate in Italy. They also serve wonderful arrays of typical cakes and pastries.

More unusual offerings in the dessert repertoire of these regions include the traditional, crumbly polenta cake, and the chewy, moist pasta cake, which is drizzled with melted chocolate.

PEAR AND AMARETTI TARTS
CROSTATE DI PERE D'AMARETTI

Crumbled amaretti cover the pastry case for these delectable little tarts, which are topped with pears and pine nuts. It is essential to use pears that are quite ripe, without being overripe, to ensure they cook to the perfect level of tenderness. Adding milk to the pastry near to the end of cooking makes it moist and crumbly and gives it a lovely golden sheen. Serve these tasty tarts warm, accompanied by a scoop of vanilla ice cream or mascarpone.

1 Preheat the oven to 180°C/350°F/Gas 4. Sift the flour and baking powder into a pile on the work surface and make a hollow in the centre with your fist.

2 Add 115g/4oz/generous ½ cup of caster sugar, the butter, egg and yolk, vanilla and salt to the hollow, then knead together to make a soft ball of dough.

3 Remove one-third of the dough and roll it into a ball. Roll the remaining two-thirds of the dough into another ball and set both balls of dough aside until required.

4 Generously grease six individual tart tins (pans) with butter, then dust each tin first with plain flour, then with breadcrumbs.

5 Roll out the larger ball of dough on a lightly floured work surface, to about 1cm/½in thick.

6 Cut out circles of dough large enough to line each of the greased tart tins, then use to line the tart tins, pressing the pastry in carefully with your fingers.

7 Cover the base of each lined case with a layer of conserve, then arrange a thick layer of the amaretti crumbs on top.

8 Arrange the pears on top of the amaretti crumbs, cutting them to fit, then sprinkle over the pine nuts and remaining caster sugar.

9 Use the smaller ball of dough to first line the edges of the top of each tart carefully, and second, to create a lattice pattern for the top of each tart.

10 Bake the tarts in the preheated oven for about 20–30 minutes, or until browned.

11 Remove the tarts from the oven, brush generously with milk, then bake for a further 8–10 minutes.

12 Remove the tarts from the tins and put each one on a serving plate. Dust lightly with a little icing sugar, then serve while still warm.

MAKES 6 INDIVIDUAL TARTS

250g/9oz/2¼ cups plain (all-purpose) flour, plus extra for dusting
10ml/2 tsp baking powder, sifted
150g/5oz/¾ cup caster (superfine) sugar
115g/4oz/½ cup unsalted butter, softened, plus extra for greasing
1 egg, plus 1 egg yolk
5ml/1 tsp vanilla extract
pinch of salt
breadcrumbs, for dusting
45ml/3 tbsp pear, peach or apricot conserve
75g/3oz amaretti, crumbled
6 small ripe pears, halved, peeled and cored
50g/2oz/½ cup pine nuts
25g/1oz/2 tbsp caster (superfine) sugar
45–60ml/3–4 tbsp full cream (whole) milk, for brushing
icing (confectioners') sugar, for dusting

> ### COOK'S TIPS
> • Although you won't get quite the same texture, you can use frozen sweet pastry, if you are very short of time.
> • If you prefer, you can make one 30cm/12in tart with the same quantity of ingredients used in this recipe. Bake for 30–40 minutes, then add the milk glaze and bake for a further 8–10 minutes.

VENETIAN FRITTERS
FRITTELLE VENEZIANE

These lovely, light and airy fritters have a gorgeous golden colour and are an important part of the street food tradition connected to Carnevale. During this festival, fried goodies are available to warm and cheer all passing revellers. All over Italy, the art of deep-frying is highly respected. People usually do this sort of cooking either outdoors or on a balcony in order to prevent the house being pervaded by the smell of frying. In Italy, the sounds and smells of the sizzling and bubbling of the frying process are often associated with the atmosphere of fun and partying. Serve these classic Venetian sweet treats with strong coffee, a chilled dessert wine or a helping of creamy ice cream.

MAKES ABOUT 28

40g/1½oz fresh yeast
50ml/2fl oz/¼ cup warm milk, plus
    2–4 tbsp extra for kneading
130g/4½oz/scant 1 cup sultanas
    (golden raisins)
25ml/1½ tbsp anise or rum
500g/1¼lb/5 cups plain (all-purpose)
    flour, sifted
75g/3oz/6 tbsp caster
    (superfine) sugar
pinch of salt
50g/2oz/½ cup pine nuts
50g/2oz/⅓ cup chopped mixed
    candied peel
grated rind of l lemon
sunflower oil, for deep-frying
icing (confectioners') sugar,
    for dusting

1 Put the yeast in a bowl and pour over the warm milk. Leave until frothy.

2 Put the sultanas in a small bowl and cover with the anise or rum. Leave to soak.

3 Put the flour and sugar in a large bowl and stir together. Make a hole in the centre and pour in the yeast mixture. Mix together thoroughly, adding as much milk as required to make a smooth, soft dough.

4 Mix in the salt, pine nuts, candied peel and lemon rind. Cover the bowl with clear film (plastic wrap) and leave the dough to rise in a warm place for about 6 hours. The dough should be very sticky and stringy at this point.

5 Mix the dough again, adding a little more milk if necessary to make the dough slightly wet – you must be able to spoon it.

6 Heat about 1 litre/1¾ pints/4 cups sunflower oil in a deep pan to 180°C/350°F, or until a small piece of bread dropped into the oil sizzles instantly and browns in about 45 seconds.

7 Fry tablespoonfuls of the fritter mixture in the hot oil, in batches. As soon as the fritters float to the surface, scoop them out of the pan using a slotted spoon and allow to drain on kitchen paper.

8 Dust the fritters with icing sugar and serve them piping hot, with coffee, if you like.

PER FRITTER Energy 150kcal/628kJ; Protein 2.1g; Carbohydrate 21.1g, of which sugars 7.5g; Fat 6.9g, of which saturates 0.8g; Cholesterol 0mg; Calcium 34mg; Fibre 0.8g; Sodium 8mg.

POTATO FRITTERS
CHIFELINI

These little fritters are a traditional sweet treat of the port city of Trieste. They are sometimes called chifeletti. They are also found all over the region of Friuli-Venezia Giulia and in neighbouring Trentino-Alto Adige. They are especially delicious when served at the end of a meal with a small glass of chilled sweet dessert wine, or as an afternoon snack with a cup of warming hot chocolate. Whatever you accompany them with, make sure they are served piping hot.

1 Boil the potatoes in plenty of water until they are tender. Drain the potatoes, remove the skin, then immediately push them through a food mill into a large mixing bowl.

2 Stir the flour into the mashed potatoes with the sugar, eggs, salt and melted butter.

3 Using a little at a time, shape the mixture into tiny crescent shapes, using extra flour to stop them sticking to your hands or the work surface.

4 Heat the oil in a pan to 180°C/350°F, or until a cube of bread sizzles instantly and browns in about 45 seconds.

5 Fry the crescents, in batches, until they are crisp and golden. Drain them thoroughly on kitchen paper.

6 Serve the fritters hot, dusted with the icing sugar and cinnamon, with cups of hot chocolate, if you like.

SERVES 4

1kg/2¼lb floury potatoes, unpeeled
200g/7oz/1¾ cups plain (all-purpose) flour, plus extra for dusting
115g/4oz/generous ½ cup caster (superfine) sugar
2 eggs, beaten
pinch of salt
20g/¾oz/1½ tbsp unsalted butter, melted
1 litre/1¾ pints/4 cups sunflower oil
30ml/2 tbsp icing (confectioners') sugar, sifted, for dusting
5ml/1 tsp ground cinnamon, for dusting

COOK'S TIP

The dough can be made in advance, if you like. Cover and put in the refrigerator, then form into crescent shapes and deep-fry when needed.

PER PORTION Energy 757kcal/3182kJ; Protein 12.3g; Carbohydrate 109.2g, of which sugars 34.1g; Fat 33.2g, of which saturates 6.8g; Cholesterol 107mg; Calcium 115mg; Fibre 4.1g; Sodium 103mg.

MAKES ABOUT 18 BISCUITS

300g/11oz/2¾ cups plain
  (all-purpose) flour
5ml/1 tsp baking powder
25g/1oz/2 tbsp unsalted butter, lard
  or vegetable oil
50g/2oz/4 tbsp soft dark
  brown sugar
15ml/1 tbsp mixed spices,
  including cinnamon, nutmeg
  and white pepper

PER BISCUIT Energy 78kcal/330kJ; Protein 1.6g;
Carbohydrate 15.9g, of which sugars 3.2g; Fat 1.4g,
of which saturates 0.8g; Cholesterol 3mg;
Calcium 25mg; Fibre 0.5g; Sodium 11mg.

VENETIAN BISCUITS
PEVARINI

When making these very traditional Venetian biscuits, you will find you need to work with an extremely stiff, hard dough. If necessary, use a food processor to help you. Pevarini keep very well for up to two months in an airtight container. Many recipes from the Veneto region, and Venice in particular, seem to reflect the need for making foods that will store for a while, presumably with the idea of sea voyaging in mind. The marine shapes of these biscuits continue this theme.

1 Preheat the oven to 190°C/375°F/Gas 5 and line a baking tray with baking parchment.

2 Sift the flour on to a work surface with the baking powder.

3 Add the butter, lard or oil, the sugar, and the spices. Knead everything together thoroughly. Roll the dough out to a thickness of 5mm/¼in.

4 With a sharp, pointed knife, cut biscuits (cookies) out of the dough in your desired shapes (traditionally fish or seahorses).

5 Arrange on the prepared baking tray and bake in the preheated oven for about 20 minutes, until golden brown.

6 Cool on racks, then serve with ice cream or dessert wine.

VENETIAN SPICED BISCUITS
FORTI

These typical Venetian biscuits will be quite soft when first baked and will gradually harden as they cool and mature. As they harden, the black treacle flavour intensifies and the colour darkens. Looking at this age-old recipe is like reading the list of available items from a 15th-century Venetian merchant! The word forti means 'hard' or 'strong' in Italian, which you will discover is not a bad name for them at all. The dough needs to be chilled in the refrigerator overnight, then baked the next day.

MAKES 40 TO 50 BISCUITS

250g/9oz/scant ¾ cup black
 treacle (molasses)
250g/9oz/1¼ cups sugar
50g/2oz/¼ cup butter,
 softened and cubed,
 plus extra for greasing
2 eggs, beaten
250g/9oz/2¼ cups almonds
90ml/6 tbsp sweet dessert wine
100g/3¾oz/scant ½ cup
 unsweetened cocoa powder
5ml/1 tsp ground cinnamon
5ml/1 tsp ground cloves
2.5ml/½ tsp ground ginger
2.5ml/½ tsp ground black pepper
5ml/1 tsp salt
15ml/1 tbsp warm milk
400–450g/14oz–1lb/3½–4 cups
 plain (all-purpose) flour
30ml/2 tbsp icing
 (confectioners') sugar
1 egg white
30–60ml/2–4 tbsp sugar crystals

1 Whisk the black treacle, sugar, butter and beaten eggs together thoroughly.

2 Pound 200g/7oz/generous 1 cup almonds using a mortar and pestle, or process them in a food processor.

3 Stir the pounded almonds into the treacle mixture. Add the wine and cocoa powder, then stir in the ground cinnamon, cloves, ginger and black pepper.

4 Stir the salt into the milk, then add this to the mixture.

5 Add enough flour to the mixture to make a stiff and kneadable dough, then wrap the dough in baking parchment and chill overnight in the refrigerator.

6 Preheat the oven to 180°C/350°F/Gas 4 and grease two baking sheets with butter.

7 Roll out the mixture into two 6cm/2½in thick tubes. Cut each one into rounds of about 2.5cm/1in thick. Push a hole in the centre of each one with your thumb or a small pastry (cookie) cutter.

8 Arrange the biscuits (cookies) on the prepared baking sheets, spreading them well apart. Pound or process the remaining almonds with the icing sugar, using a mortar and pestle or food processor.

9 Put the egg white into a clean, grease-free bowl and whisk until foaming. Combine it with the almond mixture, then use to brush over the biscuits.

10 Sprinkle with the sugar crystals and bake the biscuits for 15 minutes, or until golden. They will still be soft after this time but will firm up as they cool. Leave them on the baking tray for 1 minute to allow them to firm slightly, then transfer to wire racks to cool.

11 Store in airtight containers until required, then serve with coffee, if you like.

PER BISCUIT Energy 109kcal/459kJ; Protein 2.6g; Carbohydrate 15.5g, of which sugars 9g; Fat 4.4g, of which saturates 1.1g; Cholesterol 10mg; Calcium 55mg; Fibre 0.9g; Sodium 37mg.

SOFT PUMPKIN CAKE
TORTA DI ZUCCA

This rich, moist cake is excellent served warm with ice cream, mascarpone cheese or custard. Its texture will remain soft and squashy, making it more of a baked pudding than a cake. Traditionally, the knobbly, slightly blueish-skinned Barucca pumpkin from the Chioggia area is used to make this cake, but any kind of pumpkin will work, as long as it isn't too fibrous and stringy. What is special about this cake, apart from the flavour, is its glorious, bright orange colour.

1 Preheat the oven to 180°C/350°F/Gas 4. Grease a 20cm/8in fairly shallow cake tin (pan) and line it with baking parchment. Soak the sultanas in the grappa until swollen.

2 Put the pumpkin into a pan with the butter and cook over low heat until soft. Mash it thoroughly with a pinch of salt.

3 Stir the sugar into the pumpkin with the almonds, candied citron peel, grated rind and the sultanas with the grappa. Beat together until thoroughly mixed.

4 Sift in the flour and baking powder, and stir to mix. Beat the egg yolks until light and foamy, then fold in.

5 In a grease-free bowl, whisk the egg whites until stiff. Fold them lightly into the mixture.

6 Pour the mixture into the prepared tin and bake for 1 hour, until a wooden skewer inserted into the centre of the cake comes out clean. Leave to cool in the tin for 10 minutes, then turn out on to a wire rack. Dust with icing sugar and serve cool.

SERVES 6 TO 8

50g/2oz/⅓ cup sultanas
  (golden raisins)
45ml/3 tbsp grappa
600g/1lb 5oz pumpkin (preferably
  Barucca, see Cook's Tip), peeled
  and cubed
150g/5oz/10 tbsp unsalted butter
150g/5oz/¾ cup sugar
50g/2oz/½ cup coarsely
  ground almonds
50g/2oz/⅓ cup candied citron
  peel, chopped
grated rind of 1 lemon
75g/3oz/⅔ cup plain (all-purpose) flour
10ml/2 tsp baking powder
2 eggs, separated
vegetable oil, for greasing
icing (confectioners') sugar,
  for dusting
sea salt

> **COOK'S TIP**
>
> Barucca pumpkin may be difficult to find, so you can use butternut squash or any firm orange-fleshed winter squash instead, if you like.

PER PORTION Energy 280kcal/1164kJ; Protein 4.6g; Carbohydrate 17.4g, of which sugars 9.7g; Fat 20.6g, of which saturates 10.9g; Cholesterol 91mg; Calcium 72mg; Fibre 1.9g; Sodium 178mg.

300g/11oz/2¾ cups blanched
    almonds
300g/11oz/generous 1½ cups sugar
300g/11oz/2¾ cups fine yellow
    polenta flour
grated rind of 1 lemon
3 egg yolks
90ml/6 tbsp single (light) cream
pinch of salt
butter, for greasing
flaked (sliced) almonds,
    to decorate

PER PORTION Energy 560kcal/2345kJ; Protein 13g;
Carbohydrate 69.7g, of which sugars 41.2g; Fat 26.4g,
of which saturates 3.7g; Cholesterol 82mg;
Calcium 130mg; Fibre 3.6g; Sodium 16mg.

POLENTA CAKE
TORTA SBRISULOTTA

As the name indicates (sbrisulotta means 'crumb-like'), this is a crumbly cake, which falls apart as soon as you bite into it. It has a wonderfully granular texture, and excellent flavour. Polenta flour, generally much more widely available in the region of the Veneto than wheat flour, has many culinary uses, including cake-making. Traditional recipes for this cake exist all over the region, but this is one of the richest because of the large quantity of almonds.

1 Preheat the oven to 180°C/350°F/Gas 4. Butter a shallow 20cm/8in cake tin (pan) well.

2 Grind the almonds finely using a mortar and pestle or in a food processor, then mix them with the sugar, polenta flour and the lemon rind in a large bowl.

3 Mix in the egg yolks and the cream to make a thick but wet dough. Stir in a pinch of salt.

4 Pour into the cake tin and bake for 20 minutes, until firm and crisp. Cool in the tin, then sprinkle with flaked almonds and serve with coffee or hot chocolate, if you like.

VERONESE PASTA CAKE
TORTA DI PAPARELE ALLA VERONESE

This recipe comes from the beautiful city of Verona, which is famous for quite a few fabulous cakes. It may seem unusual to have pasta in a sweet recipe, but it works wonderfully. The end result should be moist and chewy. To save time, instead of making the pasta dough yourself, you could use ready-made, soft egg pasta cut into tiny ribbons, such as tagliolini, and then drizzle it with melted butter between the layers. Dried pasta cannot be used for this recipe.

1 Preheat the oven to 180°C/350°F/Gas 4. Put 300g/11oz/2⅔ cups flour on to the work surface. Make a hole in the centre and break in the eggs. Pour in the melted butter. Add a pinch of salt, then knead together to make a soft pasta dough.

2 Roll the dough out on a floured surface as thinly as possible.

3 Grease a 23cm/9in round cake tin (pan) thoroughly with butter, then coat the inside with the rest of the flour.

4 In a small bowl mix together the almonds, sugar and lemon rind.

5 Cut the rolled-out pasta dough into narrow even ribbons using a pasta wheel or sharp knife.

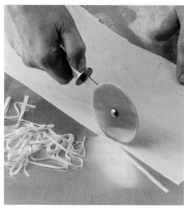

6 Arrange a layer of pasta ribbons in the base of the cake tin, then sprinkle with some of the almond mixture. Sprinkle with some of the liqueur and cover with another layer of pasta ribbons. Continue until you have used up all the ingredients, ending with pasta ribbons.

7 Cover the top of the cake with a sheet of generously buttered baking parchment and bake in the preheated oven for 55 minutes, or until golden brown.

8 Remove the cake from the oven and sprinkle with the lemon juice.

9 Run a knife around the edge of the cake, then carefully remove it from the tin.

10 Melt the chocolate in a heatproof bowl over a pan of gently simmering water, then drizzle it over the cake. Serve warm or cold.

SERVES 6 TO 8

350g/12oz/3 cups plain
  (all-purpose) flour
3 large (US extra large) eggs
50g/2oz/¼ cup unsalted butter,
  melted, plus extra for greasing
pinch of salt
200g/7oz/1¾ cups almonds,
  finely chopped
200g/7oz/1 cup sugar
grated rind of 1 lemon
90ml/6 tbsp liqueur of your choice,
  traditionally Amaretto
30ml/2 tbsp lemon juice
200g/7oz cooking chocolate

PER PORTION Energy 635kcal/2665kJ; Protein 13.1g; Carbohydrate 81.7g, of which sugars 46.4g; Fat 29g, of which saturates 9.4g; Cholesterol 88mg; Calcium 156mg; Fibre 3.2g; Sodium 84mg.

CANDIED FRUIT AND NUT ROLL
GUBANA

This is a traditional cake of Trieste, in the far north-east of Italy, which for centuries has been one of the most important Adriatic ports. Trieste is deservedly famous for its cafés and patisseries, which celebrate the culinary talents and ingredients of the Austro-Hungarian Empire. This spiral-shaped bread is filled with nuts and candied fruit, scented with grappa and enriched with butter, eggs and sugar. It's wonderful with milky coffee or hot chocolate, or at the end of a meal with a glass of chilled dessert wine.

SERVES 8

30g/1¼oz fresh yeast
675g/1½lb/6 cups plain (all-purpose) flour, plus extra for dusting
5 eggs
150g/5oz/¾ cup sugar
150g/5oz/10 tbsp unsalted butter, softened, plus extra for greasing
30ml/2 tbsp grappa
grated rind of 1 lemon
90–105ml/6–7 tbsp milk
75g/3oz/½ cup sultanas (golden raisins)
60ml/4 tbsp dessert wine
75ml/5 tbsp unblanched almonds
90ml/6 tbsp shelled walnuts
40g/1½oz/¼ cup mixed (candied) peel
40g/1½oz/¼ cup candied orange peel
30ml/2 tbsp pine nuts
grated rind of 1 orange
15ml/1 tbsp dried fine breadcrumbs
sea salt

1 Put the yeast in a bowl and mix in 75–90ml/5–6 tbsp tepid water. Stir in 115g/4oz/1 cup flour, then leave to stand for about 20 minutes.

2 Beat 3 eggs. Put them into a large bowl with the remaining flour, 115g/4oz/generous ½ cup sugar, 115g/4oz/½ cup butter, 15ml/1 tbsp grappa, a pinch of salt and the lemon rind.

3 Add the yeast and flour mixture and knead everything together. Remove the dough from the bowl and knead to form a soft dough, adding the milk to the mixture, a little at a time. You may not need to add all the milk.

4 Put the dough back into the bowl, cover with a dampened dish towel and leave to rise in a warm place for 2 hours, or until doubled in size. Meanwhile, put the sultanas into a small bowl and pour over the dessert wine to cover. Leave the sultanas to swell.

5 Put the almonds and walnuts into a small bowl and pour over enough boiling water to cover. Leave to stand for 2–3 minutes, then peel off the skins. Chop the blanched nuts and the candied peels, then put them into a bowl with the pine nuts, grated orange rind, the drained sultanas and the remaining grappa. Mix well.

6 Heat 15g/½oz/1 tbsp butter in a frying pan, add the breadcrumbs and fry until crispy. Add to the fruit mixture.

7 Preheat the oven to 190°C/375°F/Gas 5, and grease and flour a baking sheet. Separate 1 egg. Beat the egg yolk and set aside. Put the egg white into a clean, grease-free bowl and whisk until stiff. Mix the remaining egg into the fruit mixture, then fold in the egg white.

8 Knock back (punch down) the dough on a floured surface and roll out to 2cm/¾in thick. Spread the filling over the dough, then roll it up to make a spiral.

9 Transfer to the baking sheet and brush with the beaten egg yolk. Sprinkle with the remaining sugar and dot with the remaining butter. Bake for about 45 minutes, or until golden brown and cooked through.

PER PORTION Energy 787kcal/3306kJ; Protein 19.2g; Carbohydrate 102.9g, of which sugars 35.3g; Fat 34.7g, of which saturates 12.8g; Cholesterol 210mg; Calcium 240mg; Fibre 4.8g; Sodium 274mg.

INDEX

PUBLISHER'S ACKNOWLEDGEMENTS
The publishers would like to thank the
following for permission to reproduce
their images: 7tl Walter Bibikow/JAI/
Corbis; 7tr Cephas Picture Library/Alamy;
7b STF/epa/ Corbis; 8, 10bl, 12tr and 13t
CuboImages srl/ Alamy; 9tl Robert
Harding Picture Library Ltd/Alamy; 9tr and
11t Stock Italia/Alamy; 9b Kevin Galvin/
Alamy; 10br Bon Appetit/ Alamy; 11b JTB
Photo Communications, Inc./Alamy; 12tl
isifa Image Service s.r.o./ Alamy; 13t
funkyfood – London Paul Williams/Alamy;
13b Elio Ciol/Corbis; 14l JKimages/Alamy;
14r Mike Booth/Alamy; 15b PhotoDreams/
Alamy; 40r, 44r, 51l, 54r, 64r, 78r, 84r, 88r,
96r, 115l, 119l, 122r, 125l iStockphoto.

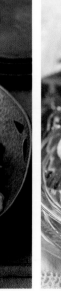